Fight the Good Fight of Faith

Playing Your Part in God's Unfolding Drama

The Sacred Roots Follow-Up Curriculum

by Rev. Don Allsman and Rev. Dr. Don L. Davis

TUMI Press
3701 East 13th Street North
Wichita, Kansas 67208

The Urban Ministry Institute • *a ministry of* World Impact, Inc.

Fight the Good Fight of Faith: Playing Your Part in God's Unfolding Drama

© 2014. The Urban Ministry Institute. All Rights Reserved. Copying, redistribution, and/or sale of these materials, or any unauthorized transmission, except as may be expressly permitted by the 1976 Copyright Act or in writing from the publisher is prohibited. Requests for permission should be addressed in writing to:

The Urban Ministry Institute
3701 East 13th Street North
Wichita, KS 67208

ISBN: 9781629323015

Published by TUMI Press
A division of World Impact, Inc.

The Urban Ministry Institute is a ministry of World Impact, Inc.

All Scripture quotations, unless otherwise noted, are from The Holy Bible, English Standard Version, copyright © 2001 by Crossway Bible. A division of Good News Publishers. Used by permission. All Rights Reserved.

This book is written in honor of

Those who disciple and mentor new and growing believers . . .

*To the pastors, teachers, mentors, spiritual directors, and disciplers –
all those who offer spiritual watch-care and friendship to these dear saints,
whose desire is constantly to strengthen and build up Christ's followers
and whose efforts to love, comfort, instruct, and strengthen them
is being used by the Holy Spirit worldwide –*

*We celebrate God's grace as they employ their gifts to raise up
a new generation of spiritually qualified laborers
to honor the Lord Jesus and to advance his Kingdom.*

• • •

To my *Fairmount Park Daybreak Crew* of years ago
that believed in the power of investing
in young urban leaders like myself for the Kingdom.

~ Don Davis

• • •

To Shirley Isaac, my 6th grade classmate who introduced me
to Jesus and the gospel, and to Theron Friberg, my high school church youth leader,
who passed on his love for the Bible and taught me to walk in the Spirit.

~ Don Allsman

• • •

*And what you have heard from me in the presence of many witnesses
entrust to faithful men who will be able to teach others also.*

~ 2 Timothy 2.2 (ESV)

TABLE OF CONTENTS

Appendix

INTRODUCTION

> Discipleship is not a communication of knowledge, but a communication of life.
>
> ~ Juan Carlos Ortiz

Greetings, fellow soldiers, in the strong name of our Lord Jesus Christ!

It is our pleasure to offer you our resource for the growing disciple/warrior of Christ, *Fight the Good Fight of Faith: Playing Your Part in God's Unfolding Drama*. This lesson book represents our sketch of the drama of the Scriptures, written with a focus on learning what the Bible itself has to say about the key dimensions of our participation in God's grand Story. We are convinced that the true Story of the world, its purpose and destiny, is recorded in the Bible. The Scriptures show God as the author of life, creating the universe, and making a promise to Abraham to send a Seed who would bless all the families of the earth. God made himself known to his people Israel, that nation through which he brought the Messiah, his anointed one. Jesus was the Servant chosen by God to come into the world, to defeat death, end the Curse, and establish his reign among humankind.

In truth, the Messiah did come through his people, Israel, and we know who he is: the Redeemer and King, Jesus of Nazareth. The Scriptures testify of the glory of Jesus, the One who revealed to all humankind the Father's plan and glory, redeemed us from our sins by his death on the Cross and his resurrection from the dead, and who will soon restore all things upon his Second Coming again. When we repent and believe in Jesus as Lord and Savior, this grand Story becomes our very own, an amazing tale of grace and love, a wonderful drama that he invites us to share and to live with others in God's very own family, the church.

Lesson Overview: How to Fight the Good Fight of Faith

This book is written in order to offer the reader a clear, easy-to-comprehend overview of the big questions and highlights of that Story, to help you understand it so you can know how to relate to God and to others as you live it in the church. It is meant to give to you, a hungry, growing believer, nine integrated lessons that lay out the key elements of the Story, carefully considering each one and discussing it as it relates to you as a new actor in the Cosmic Story of God. Discussing specific truths outlined by the apostle Paul in the book of Ephesians, the lessons are designed to ground you in the basics of the Christian faith and walk. Here are the lesson titles, and a brief description of each lesson.

Lesson 1 is entitled *The Epic We Find Ourselves In: Joining Our Story with the Story of God*. This lesson helps you know that the God of the universe, the Lord God Almighty, is the one, true, and everlasting God, existing in three Persons: Father, Son, and Holy Spirit. He created all things, visible and invisible, and made human beings in his own image. This lesson discusses the rebellion of Satan and the first human pair, Adam and Eve, and how through their disobedience all creation was cursed. God, however, gives us a promise of a Savior who would overcome evil and win everything back for God's glory.

Lesson 2, *The Enlistment We Make: Accepting Our Role in the Cosmic Conflict of the Ages*, discusses how Jesus of Nazareth defeated the devil and set us free from the Curse through his sinless life and dying in our place. Now through repentance (turning to God from our sins) and faith (believing the truth concerning the work of Jesus), we enter God's Kingdom. He saves us by his grace, we are baptized into the Body of Christ, and we are given the Holy Spirit to help us in our Christian life.

Lesson 3, *The Entrance We Get: Linking Our Life with the Life of God in Christ*, teaches you how you are joined to Jesus by faith (i.e., we are now "in Christ"). Because of this union, you receive and experience all that Jesus is and provides. Through God's Spirit, we become members of his household, with Jesus Christ as its cornerstone, and the apostles and prophets as its foundation. Every local assembly of believers functions as an embassy of God's Kingdom, representing the interests of heaven itself. We believers serve as ambassadors and agents of that Kingdom.

Lesson 4 is entitled *The Endowment We Receive: The Holy Spirit's Role in the Good Fight of Faith*. This lesson highlights how the Holy Spirit indwells every believer, granting to each one gifts to serve the church. We are free in Christ to exercise our gifts among other believers, as the Holy Spirit provides the opportunity, direction, and strength. We grow together as every believer serves the fellowship in unity and love.

In **Lesson 5**, *The Excellence We Show: Living as Saints of God and Ambassadors of Christ in This World*, we see that we are called to imitate God, as his own dearly loved children. We have been made God's saints (holy ones) in Christ, and are to represent God before others as his own holy, thankful people. We are also called as his ambassadors, to share the Good News of salvation with our friends, families, and neighbors, and do good works of love, works for Christ, in service to others.

Lesson 6, *The Edification We Seek: Building up One Another in the Body of Christ* explores the idea of the Christian life as being designed to live in community, growing together as God's family, being the body of Christ and the temple of the Holy Spirit. We are called to live the life of Christ together with others, discovering his truth together, worshiping God and growing as disciples of Christ as we relate to other believers in the local church and in small groups. In doing this we are built up (edified) in our faith, and come to learn how to submit to each other out of reverence (respect) for Christ.

Lesson 7, *The Enemy We Fight: Walking in Victory Against the Enemy of God*, describes the nature of the grand Story we have joined. The universe is at spiritual war – the devil and the kingdom of darkness are battling against the Lord Jesus Christ and the Kingdom of light. Through his life, death, and resurrection, Jesus won the victory over our enemy, the devil, who still continues to work through deception in this fallen world system and our old sinful nature, i.e., "the desires of the flesh." We overcome him as we walk by faith in Christ, and stay watchful for the devil's attempt to deceive us through lies and deception.

Lesson 8 is entitled *The Equipment We Use: Putting on the Whole Armor of God*. It explains how God has provided every believer with the necessary armor to resist the enemy and stand their ground when under attack. The truth of Scripture (i.e., the Word of God) can enable us to identify, stand against, and replace the lies that the enemy hurls against us, and the Holy Spirit strengthens us for the fight as we practice the spiritual disciplines, alone and together with other believers.

Lesson 9 is our final lesson, called *The Endurance We Display: The Perseverance of the Saints*. In this lesson we see how the central principle of growing up into Christ is learning to persevere, to stay alert, and not get caught off guard. As representatives of Christ, we must press on and continue forward for the prize, no matter how hard it may become. The Holy Spirit will give us power to stand true to our calling, and as we faithfully represent Christ, he will use us to strengthen other believers in their fight.

Blueprint for Each Lesson: Its Parts and Elements

Each lesson is divided into the same particular parts, with each element focusing on something necessary for you to attend as you go through it. (This is especially important to note if you wind up going through this book with others, as a leader or small group facilitator).

Lesson Objectives. These goals, three for each lesson, will help you understand exactly what you are to understand and believe once you finish the lesson, whether you are studying alone or with others.

Opening Prayer for Wisdom. This prayer, which we encourage you to recite and pray aloud, asks the Lord to prepare our hearts before we enter into our study of the Bible truths, so we can both understand and receive what the Lord has for us.

Contact. The Contact section is a "prime the pump" section that allows you to get started into the lesson by pondering real-life questions, issues, and situations that relate to its ideas. Spend good time on these examples, and think through carefully the implications of these issues. They will sharpen your thinking and research as you move forward into each lesson.

Content. The Content section gives an introductory explanation of the material we are about to study, and provides the actual questions and biblical references we will answer and look up for that particular lesson.

Appendices. We have created and included appropriate graphics, articles, and documents in the Appendix that can greatly enhance your ability to comprehend and apply the content in the lessons. Refer to the Appendices included in this section, as they are relevant to enriching your under-standing of the root principles and ideas in each particular lesson.

Summary. After looking up Scriptures, and answering questions in the Content section, each lesson provides you with a short, compact summary of the key ideas and truths that the Content was meant to explore. This is helpful as a guide for you, to check whether or not you got the "big ideas" of the lesson in your personal study of the Scriptures.

Key Principle. This section of the lesson usually brings together the entire teaching of the lesson under a single sentence or verse.

Case Studies. This important section, provides an opportunity for you to reflect on the implications of your learning in the context of possible and actual cases. Truth is not simply for the sake of thinking and discussion; discipleship is about real life, real issues that people are wrestling with, that impact and affect their lives. They are meant to provoke your thinking, and help you, as a growing disciple, understand how to relate the Story and its truth to your stories and truths. Knowing the truth is not to make us smart, but to set us free (John 8.31-32).

What is more important than "the right answer" is "the humble learning." You will see in studying the Bible that often no one, clear, right answer emerges from our research. Rather, we are called to reflect, to humbly engage in study, to test everything, and to hold on to that which is good (1 Thess. 5.21). Use these cases to explore possible meanings of what you have just learned, and be open to letting the Spirit change the way in which you understand the different issues you will encounter in the lessons.

Connection. This section focuses on your application and actualization ("acting upon") of the truths of the lesson. You must connect what you learn with the ways in which you think, speak, conduct yourself, and relate to others. Therefore, look for possible ways to link what you are learning to your personal life in this section.

Affirmation. This concise section includes a truth drawn from the materials in the lesson that we can and should confess and affirm throughout the week.

Prayer. We include a prayer from a key figure in the Church, to give you a sense of the kinds of petitions and prayers that have been offered connected with our lesson themes throughout church history.

Heart Cry to God. This is a prayer that you should pray at the end of the lesson. Prayers can be drafted and written (like those of the Psalms in the Bible)! These prayers help us to ask the Lord for the particular grace we need to receive and embody the truths he has taught us in this lesson. They are prayers of humility, supplication, and confidence. Pray them, silently and out loud, as the Spirit leads you.

For More Study. These items are suggestions for you if you desire to learn more on the subject covered in a lesson.

For the Next Session. These items preview the subjects and themes of the next lesson in the series, and offer you a nice, concise look at what's ahead in the next session.

Scripture Memory. We strongly believe that if we hide the Word (memorize it) in our hearts, we will not sin against the Lord (Ps. 119.11). Knowing the Word by heart is an effective encouragement of the heart, and a ready resource against the lies of the enemy. Therefore, each lesson will contain a single memory verse, so you can commit to memory at least one biblical text that can remind you of the truth you learned, and aid you in your walk during the week and the weeks to come.

Assignments. This final section, contains specific "take aways" and tasks for you to do as you complete the lesson. These are meant to be helpful and practical. If you will act on these assignments, take them seriously, and strive to do them thoroughly and excellently, your learning of the material will multiply greatly. They are designed to help you grow up in Christ, informed by the light of the lesson you just studied. So, please, complete the assignments, and follow through on them promptly. It will enhance your learning greatly if you do not simply think about these truths, but actually put them into practice.

Fight the Good Fight of Faith: Playing Your Part in God's Unfolding Drama (The Sacred Roots Follow-up Curriculum)

To become a Christian is to join the Story of God, a Story that God is telling and fulfilling through all time! His story of redemption and love, of salvation and hope, of battle and victory, has now become your Story. The sacred roots of this Story go back to the beginning of time, and extend to the hope of the glorious Kingdom under Christ's reign. Through faith in the Lord Jesus, you have been delivered from sin, released from punishment and bondage, and enlisted in the fight. In this lesson book you will find out how to put on the whole Armor of God, recognize the lies of the enemy, and learn to grow with fellow believers. You have been enrolled in the fight, so, learn how to fight the good fight, knowing that the battle for spiritual victory belongs to the Lord.

John Eldredge, a pastor who has written much on spiritual warfare, says that "The story of your life is the story of a long and brutal assault on your heart by the one who knows what you could be – and fears it." Who knows what God has in store for you as you learn to represent Christ before your family and friends, your associates and neighbors. You must learn to do battle. This is a "follow up" curriculum, designed to help you know how to start the Christian life with the right perspective and tools to fight the good fight. This guide book will show you how.

Stu Webber, a retired military officer and now a pastor, has written on the nature of the spiritual conflict that every Christian, whether young in the Lord or a seasoned warrior, faces each day:

> Stu Webber. *Spirit Warriors.* Sisters, OR: Multnomah Publishers, 2001, p. 16.

Every Christian is a walking battlefield. Every believer carries deep within himself a terrible conflict. And most of us will gravitate to anything that will help us win the battle. Call it the battle between the flesh and the spirit. Call it the quest for the victorious Christian life. Call it what you want. But it's a flat-out-knock-down-drag-out war. And when it's over, you want to be among those who are still standing. The principles of war are taught in military academies all over the world. In most ways, spiritual warfare is no different than physical warfare. Every soldier who expects to not only survive but win must understand and employ these principles in his own daily battles "against the powers of this dark world and against the spiritual forces of evil in the heavenly realms" (Ephesians 6.12b NIV).

You can do more than survive. You can win, and in your victory, Christ will be honored. Ask God to give you wisdom and strength as you learn the truths of his Word. Ask for insight to understand his truth, for boldness to apply it to your life, and for love to share it with others. We invite you to learn with us, to learn from the Spirit, as he instructs you to fight the good fight of faith. On behalf of Don Allsman, my co-author and fellow soldier, and our entire TUMI staff, who contributed time and effort to this project – we thank God for your life. Our sincere prayer is that you would play your part in God's grand Story of rescue and restoration of his creation. You have an important role to play.

Welcome to the family, welcome to the fight!

Dr. Don L. Davis
Wichita, Kansas, Advent 2014

THE EPIC WE FIND OURSELVES IN
Joining Our Story with the Story of God

> . . . according to the riches of his grace, which he lavished upon us, in all wisdom and insight, making known to us the mystery of his will, according to his purpose, which he set forth in Christ as a plan for the fulness of time, to unite all things in him, things in heaven and things on earth.
>
> ~ Ephesians 1.8-10

Objectives

By the end of this session, you should embrace the *Epic We Find Ourselves In* by believing that:

- The God of the universe, the Lord God Almighty, is the one, true, and everlasting God, existing in three Persons: Father, Son, and Holy Spirit.
- God is the Creator of all things, visible and invisible, and made human beings in his own image.
- Because of the rebellion of *Satan** and the first *human pair**, creation was cursed, but God gave a promise and has a plan to overcome evil and win everything back through a Savior, the Lord Jesus Christ.

Opening Prayer for Wisdom

Eternal God, my Father, you say in your Word that you are the source of all knowledge and wisdom. I acknowledge this as the truth, dear Father, and I ask that you impart into me divine wisdom, that I may be able to rightly divide the Word of truth (2 Timothy 2.15). Please instruct and teach me in the way I should go (Psalm 32.8), and direct my steps. Incline my ear to hear your voice, and correct me now in the way I think and speak, and lead me when I have gone astray.

Father, grant me the gift of discernment, and enable me as I study to know the difference between godly and ungodly teachings, spirits, and gifts. Show me by the Holy Spirit what your will is, and give me insight into how I can carry out your intentions with my whole heart.

....

*Satan – Satan is the personal name of the devil, the adversary of God and humankind.

*Human pair – Adam and Eve were created by God as the first man and woman, created in the image of God to be in relationship with God, do meaningful work, and enjoy the richness of God's perfect world.

Dear Lord, please help me to be quick to hear and listen, slow to speak, and slow to anger (James 1.19). Let the words of my mouth and the thoughts of my heart be acceptable in your sight. Allow me to speak your truth with wisdom in order that all with whom I speak may understand and benefit by your truth.

Teach me now in this study as I receive your Word and instruction. I ask for these things in the strong name of Jesus, my Lord and Savior, Amen.

Contact

*Divinities –
Divinities are
supernatural
beings or gods
having great
power.

1. **Are we the only ones in the universe?** Many Hollywood movies show alien life in the universe, usually associated with negative or evil things. Thousands of people believe that we are not alone in the universe, although they would quickly suggest that they have no idea where that life is, or what it is. Others believe that humankind is by itself in the vast sea of suns and galaxies of the heavenly bodies. Some believe we formed through merely natural processes, others by means of *divinities**, others strongly suggest no one can ever know such things. In growing up from childhood, what were your views on where we came from, and what ideas were you taught about the origins of the heavens and the world?

2. **"Once upon a time . . . !"** Most of us grew up hearing stories as a child–nursery rhymes, fairy tales, and other stories designed for children, taught at home, in church, or at school. Wherever human beings live in the world, they love to hear and tell stories. Films, books, comedians, tv shows, documentaries, social media, newspapers, and radio – every day we hear dozens of stories, some true, some false, some inspiring, others shameful. Would it surprise you that the Bible itself tells a single, grand story? The Scriptures are a library of books (66 books in all, written by many authors over 1500 years) but they tell a single story – of God and his desire to save his creation.

   What do you think about stories in general? Have you ever heard that the Bible tells a single story about God and his salvation? What are some of the differences between many of the stories we have heard about or read about, and the single story being told by the authors of the Bible about God and his offer of salvation to the world?

3. **"As far as I can tell, I can't see a plan."** Since the beginning of the faith, shortly after the time of the apostles, believers have affirmed their basic belief system in the statements called creeds. Two of the most recognized and recited throughout history and even to this day are the Apostles' Creed and the Nicene Creed (see Appendix). These two concise confessions of the faith summarize the biblical vision of who God is, what he has

done in Christ, and how the creation will be restored, according to God's time and method.

Many people who do not believe, however, argue that the cosmos (the universe), was formed accidentally with no purpose or purpose-er who called it into existence. They say no plan exists that connects everything together, and there is no single explanation to help us know why we are here, where we are going, and how everything will turn out. Atheists (those who deny that there is a God) say that it is foolish to think that there is either a God or some larger plan for life. They would argue that, since there is no God but rather only the stuff of the universe that exists, there is no destiny or purpose for life and the world. Agnostics (those who say that we can never know if there is a God) say that, even if God exists, we can't know him/it/her, and the best we can do is to hope that things might turn out alright – maybe! How do the Apostles' and Nicene Creeds help us answer the objections of those who argue there is neither a God nor a plan for the universe?

Content

In the Bible we discover the Story of God and mankind, centered on Jesus Christ our Lord. But this epic Story is more than an account that we read about; it is something we participate in. As a follower of Jesus, you now have a new identity and you play a role in the *Epic We Find Ourselves In.*

The universe was created by the *sovereign** and *triune** God: Father, Son, and Holy Spirit. Living before time, dwelling in eternal glory, and lacking nothing, God chose to make a world where human beings, made in his own likeness and image, could experience the fullness of his creation. But this universe was thrown into chaos by a rebellious *angelic** prince, Satan. With the intent to overthrow God's Kingdom, the devil tempted the first human pair (Adam and Eve) to rebel against God, leaving humanity cursed and without hope of deliverance.

In the face of this rebellion, God determined to raise up a Victor, a Redeemer, who would remedy this fall and end forever the effects of the Curse. Through Abraham, God made a covenant promise to bring this Messiah (anointed one), and raised up a people out of which the Messiah

. . . .

*sovereign – Sovereign refers to unlimited power with control over the affairs of nature and history.

*triune – Triune is another way of saying "three persons but one God." Sometimes the word "Trinity" is used to refer to One God but three persons.

*angelic – Angels are supernatural beings created by God having greater power and intelligence than humans.

would come (Israel). And, in the fullness of time, the Father sent the Son, Jesus, to reveal his glory, redeem his people, and rescue his creation. Jesus displayed the Kingdom's wisdom in his teaching and power through his miracles. In voluntarily giving his life by dying on a cross, he paid the penalty for our *sin** and destroyed the devil's works. God raised Jesus from the dead, and forty days later he *ascended to heaven** as victorious Lord. On the fiftieth day after his resurrection, he then sent the Holy Spirit to empower the growing company of Jesus' *disciples**, the *Church**. As the family of the Father, the body of Christ, and the temple of the Holy Spirit, the Church is appointed to invite people everywhere to join in this Epic Story. When our good fight of faith is finished, Jesus will return to establish God's Kingdom throughout the entire universe, where sorrow, disease, and death will end and he will reign forever with his people. Glory to his name!

> Especially ought those questions to burn when we turn to the biblical story, in which the ingredient of reversal is doubled and tripled. To turn a page in that book of stories and Story which is the Bible is to confront reversal again and again. As one of us has written elsewhere, 'At the crucial moments when God displayed his mighty acts in history to reveal his nature and will, God *also* intervened to liberate the poor and oppressed.' The moments of intervention are also moments of reversal, moments when what one might expect is not what one gets, when those the world deems insignificant prove to be precisely the ones the Creator of the world deems important.
>
> ~ Ronald J. Sider and Michael A. King.
> *Preaching About Life in a Threatening World.*
> Philadelphia: The Westminster Press, 1987, pp. 56-57.

. . . .

*sin – Sin is failure to do what God desires, either by what we say, what we do, or what we think.

*ascended to heaven – Jesus physically left the earth and went into the sky as his followers looked on. After his death and resurrection, his ascension was a triumphant expression of leaving this earth to sit on his throne in heaven as victorious king. It also set in motion the coming of the Holy Spirit, who could empower Christians everywhere, all over the world.

*disciples – A disciple is a student or follower of Jesus. Every Christian is a disciple. Sometimes the term "disciple" is used in a specific way to refer to the twelve men that Jesus chose to join in his earthly ministry.

*Church – The Church is the community of God's people who acknowledge Jesus as Lord, who carry out his purposes on earth, comprised of everyone past, present and future, from every place on the earth and throughout history.

> Apart from Christ, the Bible is a closed book. Read with him at the center, it is the greatest story ever told. The Bible is trivialized when it is reduced to life's instruction manual. According to the apostles – and Jesus himself – the Bible is an unfolding drama with Jesus Christ as its central character.
>
> ~ Michael Horton. *Christless Christianity*.
> Grand Rapids, MI: Baker Books, 2008, page 142.

The Epic We Find Ourselves In
Lesson 1 Bible Study

Read the following Scriptures and answer briefly the questions associated with each biblical teaching.

1. *The LORD God alone is God, and he is the creator of the universe.* Read Genesis 1.1-3.15.

   a. What part does God play in this Story?

   b. What part do Adam and Eve play in this Story?

   c. What part does the serpent play in this Story?

2. *All peoples were formed by and exist through God's will and power.* Read Acts 17.24-31. List at least three things Paul explains about the Story of God as he talks to the Athenians.

3. *God has spoken to all humankind through his creation, through the prophets of Israel, and finally, in these last days through Jesus Christ.* Read Hebrews 1.1-4

   a. How does the writer describe the way God has spoke to humankind?

   b. What importance does the writer to the Hebrews give to God speaking to us through Jesus?

4. *God has joined the story by becoming a human being and living on the earth!* Read John 1.1-14.

    a. Who is the "Word," and what is his relationship to God?

    b. What is the relationship of the Word to all creation?

    c. For those who believe in the Word, what do they receive, and how are they "born"?

5. *The story of God's love given in Jesus is to be told to all peoples, everywhere.* Read Matthew 28.18-20. What command does Jesus give his followers?

6. *The Gospel is the Good News of salvation that summarizes the epic in which we live.* Read 1 Corinthians 15.1-8. What does Paul say is of first importance?

    a. What is "grace," and why is the Gospel (Good News) always about "grace"?

    b. The Gospel is a message about what God did in Christ. What happened?

    c. After Jesus finished his work, who did he reveal himself to?

7. *Jesus of Nazareth is the center of God's Story – his life, death, and resurrection.* Read Mark 1.1-13. When Jesus was baptized, match how God showed up as Father, Son, and Holy Spirit.

    a. Father   ___The form of a Dove

    b. Son   ___Voice from heaven

    c. Holy Spirit   ___Jesus of Nazareth

8. *The Story that God is telling in Jesus is a story of restoration, healing, and blessing to the hurting and the poor.* Read Isaiah 61.1-4. List five predictions that Isaiah says Jesus will do when he comes to win back what was lost.

My name is Nee. It is a fairly common Chinese name. How did I come by it? I did not choose it. I did not go through the list of possible Chinese names and select this one. That my name is Nee is in fact not my doing at all, and, moreover, nothing I can do can alter it. I am a Nee because my father was a Nee, and my father was a Nee because my grandfather was a Nee. If I act like a Nee I am a Nee, and if I act unlike a Nee I am still a Nee. If I become president of the Chinese Republic I am a Nee, or if I become a beggar in the street I am still a Nee. Nothing I do or refrain from doing will make me other than a Nee.

We are sinners, not because of ourselves but because of Adam. It is not because I individually have sinned that I am a sinner, but because I was in Adam when he sinned. Because by birth I came of Adam, therefore I am part of him. What is more, I can do nothing to alter this. I cannot, by improving my behavior, make myself other than a part of Adam, and so a sinner.

~ Watchman Nee. *The Normal Christian Life.*
Fort Washington, PA: Christian Literature Crusade, 1974, p. 26.

Summary

According to the Bible, the Lord God of the Hebrews is the one true God, who has revealed himself as one God in three persons (the Father, Son, and Holy Spirit). God has told us his grand story (i.e., epic) which speaks of his love and determination to save his creation from doom. God is the creator of the universe, who made all things from nothing (*ex nihilo*), and decided that he would raise up a people through whom a Leader and Savior would come. Although he originally made his people without sin, they rebelled against him, *fell from his grace**, and brought upon all creation and human-kind a curse, that ends in death. God promised to send a Savior who would pay the price of our sins, take on himself the penalty for our disobedience, and give us eternal life through faith. Jesus of Nazareth is this Savior, who

. . . .

*fell from his grace – When Adam and Eve joined Satan in rebellion, their sin separated them from God's perfect relationship; their actions alienated them from God, and brought death to the world.

died to set us free. Now, by faith in him, we can be saved from the penalty and power of sin, and receive eternal life – we can join the Story that God is telling!

Appendices

The Appendices you should study and meditate upon relevant to this lesson are the following:

Once Upon a Time (App. 1)
The Story God Is Telling (App. 2)
From Before to Beyond Time (App. 6)
The Shadow and the Substance (App. 7)
Jesus Christ, the Subject and Theme of the Bible (App. 22)
The Nicene Creed (App. 24 and 25)
The Apostles' Creed (App. 26)

> All the world is a stage, it has been said. In no sense is this more true than in the great drama being played out which we might call the 'Conflict of the Ages.' The plot in Scripture and history reveals a cosmic war between two kingdoms in which we are all playing a part according to God's plan. It is against this backdrop of God's Kingdom purpose in history that biblical writers have both written and interpreted Scripture.
>
> ~ James DeYoung and Sarah Hurty. *Beyond the Obvious*. Gresham, OR: Vision House Publishing, 1995, pp. 83-84.

Key Principle

God Almighty came to earth in Jesus of Nazareth, and reconciled the world to himself through his death on the Cross (2 Corinthians 5.19).

Case Studies

Read and reflect upon the following cases and concepts, and provide answers and insights into their resolution, based on the texts you studied above.

1. **"I don't think there is a God."** At work during lunch, Janice was discussing the idea of how the world came to be with her co-worker, Leah. Leah strongly believes that there is no evidence at all that God, or any god, exists in the world. All the religions have different ideas of who God is, how many gods there are, and what they count as sacred writings. Janice is a believer in Christ who believes that the Father

Almighty made the world, and that creation is too beautiful and magnificent for it just to have happened, without any purpose or meaning. If you were Janice, how would you share with Leah about the Scriptures you have just studied on what the Bible says about God and his creation of the world.

2. **"Why doesn't God change things now?"** In a Bible Study with some new Christians, the question came up "If God is the creator, and he is working all things together, why does horrible stuff happen in the world?" Some believed that God didn't know about all the stuff going on in the world, while others said that God knew, but he had decided not to interfere with the things going on. Based on what you know now, how would you answer the question on why things are going on now in the world as they are? How does what we learned in this lesson help us understand why God might allow us to go through hard things, at least for a time?

3. **Aren't there many paths to God?** Many people today believe that all religions are equally important and that there are many different paths that lead to God. It is as if at the bottom of a mountain, many different groups start out to hike to the top of the mountain, beginning from different points in the foothills. They all intend to get to the top of the mountain (where the "divine" lives), but they will take different paths, coming from different angles and viewpoints along the way. Sooner or later (so the argument goes) all of the hikers (the religions of the world) will find their way to the top (spirituality and the divine). In this view, all religions are equal, all speak truly of the divine, and any of them can be followed to find God. How does our study speak to this kind of reasoning about many paths to the divine?

Connection

Now that you have repented (turned away from sin) and believed in Jesus of Nazareth as Lord, you have been born from above, made a child of God through faith in the Gospel. This means that you have been chosen by God, and are a part of his grand plan to save out of humankind a people for his own glory. You are not simply reading about God's plan and Story, you have now joined it! You now have been joined to Jesus by faith, and have been forgiven of your sin, adopted into his family, and recruited into his army. When you believed in Jesus, you joined the Story!

This means you now need to learn all about the Story, what God is doing, how he wants you to live, and how you can be used by him to help others join his Story of love and salvation, too. Don't be afraid; God has given you his own Holy Spirit to teach you, he has given you the Word of God to instruct you, the Christian church to befriend you, and the power of prayer to help you get all you need to live out this great Story in your new life.

You now have new friends, as well as new enemies! You have been rescued from the power of darkness, and now you must learn to resist the lies of the devil, the temptations of the world, and the habits of your old sin nature. To be saved is to have taken God's side in a struggle, for the hearts and minds of people everywhere. But, don't worry! God has granted to us all that we need to live the Christian life, to please and glorify God, and to overcome the enemy in this great Story we now participate in.

Spend some time thanking God for drawing you to himself, for making you his child, and granting you eternal life. Ask him for strength and help to continue to learn and to grow as a disciple (follower) of Jesus, and as a soldier in his army. He will never leave nor forsake us.

Welcome to the family, and welcome to the fight!

Affirmation

I am created in the image of God, and although I was once an enemy of God, I am chosen to participate in God's cosmic plan to win back all that was lost at the fall.

Prayer

The Lord's Prayer has been used by the church for centuries, based on the Lord Jesus' own teaching to his disciples in Matthew 6.9-13 and Luke 11.2-4.

Father in heaven, hallowed by your name. Your kingdom come, your will be done in earth as it is in heaven. Give us this day our daily bread and forgive us our debts as we forgive our debtors. And lead us not into temptation but deliver us from evil. For yours is the kingdom and the power and the glory forever. Amen.

Heart Cry to the Lord

Eternal God, my Father, thank you for revealing to me your great plan and Story in the Scriptures. You created the universe and the world, and you are my maker and my God. Thank you for opening up my heart to hear the Gospel of your salvation, of the offer of eternal life you make to all people who believe in Jesus. I accept that you love me, and saved me. You have made me a part of your Story. Help me, by your Spirit, to learn how to live so I can glorify you – standing my ground against those things that would draw me away from you, and back to the world. Give me grace to please you today. In Jesus' name, amen.

For More Study

*At **www.tumi.org/sacredroots**, we have a section dedicated to additional written and video resources.*

Norman Geisler. *To Understand the Bible Look for Jesus.* Eugene, OR: Wipf and Stock Publishers, 2002.

For the Next Session

In the next session, you will explore ***The Enlistment We Make*** including these topics:

1. Jesus defeated the devil and made a way for us to join God's Kingdom.
2. Through our repentance and faith, by God's grace we are baptized into the body of Christ.
3. We have been given the Holy Spirit as a guarantee of our inheritance.

Scripture Memory

1 John 3.8

Assignments

1. On a separate paper, summarize the Story of the Bible. Share your summary with a mature believer in your church.
2. Read the Appendix "How to Start Reading the Bible".
3. Begin a daily Bible reading plan.

THE ENLISTMENT WE MAKE
Accepting Our Role in the Cosmic Conflict of the Ages

> In him you also, when you heard the word of truth, the gospel of your salvation, and believed in him, were sealed with the promised Holy Spirit, who is the guarantee of our inheritance until we acquire possession of it, to the praise of his glory.
>
> ~ Ephesians 1.13-14

Objectives

By the end of this session, you should embrace the *Enlistment We Make* by believing that:

- Through his sinless life and dying in our place, Jesus defeated the devil and made a way for those who believe to enter God's Kingdom.
- Through repentance (turning to God from our sins) and faith (believing the truth concerning the work of Jesus), and by God's grace we are baptized into the Body of Christ.
- We have been given the Holy Spirit as a guarantee of our inheritance.

Opening Prayer for Wisdom

Eternal God, my Father, you say in your Word that you are the source of all knowledge and wisdom. I acknowledge this as the truth, dear Father, and I ask that you impart into me divine wisdom, that I may be able to rightly divide the Word of truth (2 Timothy 2.15). Please instruct and teach me in the way I should go (Psalm 32.8), and direct my steps. Incline my ear to hear your voice, and correct me now in the way I think and speak, and lead me when I have gone astray.

Father, grant me the gift of discernment, and enable me as I study to know the difference between godly and ungodly teachings, spirits, and gifts. Show me by the Holy Spirit what your will is, and give me insight into how I can carry out your intentions with my whole heart.

Dear Lord, please help me to be quick to hear and listen, slow to speak, and slow to anger (James 1.19). Let the words of my mouth and the thoughts of my heart be acceptable in your sight. Allow me to speak your truth with wisdom in order that all with whom I speak may understand and benefit by your truth.

Teach me now in this study as I receive your Word and instruction. I ask for these things in the strong name of Jesus, my Lord and Savior, Amen.

Contact

1. **"Why does the devil hate us – we didn't do anything to him, did we?"** In a small group Bible study for new believers, a group of new, baby Christians were going over the Story of the Bible with their instructor. During the course of the study, they found out that the devil deceived with lies and falsehoods the first human pair, Adam and Eve, causing them to sin. One of the students asked the instructor, "I don't get it. Why was the devil so mean as to lie to Adam and Eve, get them into trouble, and mess everything up. What did they do to him – why does he hate people so much?" Based on what you know right now about the Bible and the Story, why do you think the Scriptures declare that the devil accuses, deceives, and persecutes human beings so much? Why has he done so from the very beginning?

2. **"Sure, I believe, but I don't think I'm ready to go all in – at least, not yet."** When Marsha shared the Good News of God's offer of eternal life with her cousin Ralph, she ran into something she didn't know what to do with. He told Marsha that God's offer seemed cool, even attractive, except the part about turning to God from his sins. (Ralph was deeply involved in online gaming, some of which were into black arts and shared a kind of demonic struggle storyline.) In hearing Marsha's testimony about the story, Ralph said, "I really see how much God loved us in sending Jesus – it is an amazing thing. But, honestly, right now, I don't think I can commit to him, especially if it means I've got to change everything and give up some of the stuff I'm doing right now. That's hard. Can't I simply believe in Jesus and that be enough? Why do I have to, as you were saying, "repent from my sins?" I don't think I'm ready for that kind of extreme commitment yet. Is there another way, a way to avoid all of that repentance stuff?" How should Marsha answer Ralph about this point – do you need to repent from sin in order to be saved? Explain.

3. **"Now that you're a disciple of Jesus, you've become a target."** While many people speak of Christian faith as only God's love and grace, few seem to understand faith as enlistment to God's side in a battle. The truth is, the very moment a person repents and believes in Jesus, they are involved in a war, what one Christian author called "the mother of all battles." To say "Yes!" to Christ and his Kingdom is to simultaneously say "No!" to the temptations of the world, to the inner passions of our old sinful nature, and to the lies of the enemy. Many of these lies have shaped who we are – we've believed in them our whole lives long. To become a Christian is to become a soldier, and to become a target of

God's enemies. In what ways have you found this to be true since the time you first accepted Christ Jesus as your Savior and Lord?

Content

In the last session (***The Epic We Find Ourselves In***), we learned that the Story of God's salvation in Christ, articulated in the Bible, answers the big questions about life. But as amazing as this Epic is, this grand Story must not just be heard simply for amusement, as when you go to a movie, view it, and then forget about it. When we hear God's story of rescue and restoration in Christ, then we must make a decision to cooperate with God. We must receive his testimony about his Story, accept it as the truth, let it become our very own story, and then begin to participate in this good fight of faith. We must *change sides*, voluntarily enlisting in the Lord's army.

Through no merit of our own, and completely by the mercy of God through Christ's substitutionary ("in our place") death, he extends to all humans the invitation to enlist. The invitation to be saved is a call to war – to go from the kingdom of darkness to the kingdom of light, to move from a life lived for yourself alone to becoming an ambassador of Jesus Christ as Lord, following him in the midst of a crooked and mixed-up world.

***repentance** – To repent means to change your mind, to turn around and go the other way, to go back the way God desires. When you repent, you agree with God that you were on the wrong track and change your behavior to be in line with God's will.*

If you confess your rebellion and sin, turn away from it in *repentance**, and ask for God's forgiveness through Jesus' death on the cross, God cleanses you and puts you in right relationship with him. You are placed into the Body of Christ, God's family, the Church. Upon salvation, God the Holy Spirit makes his home in us, and he then empowers us day by day to honor God, to serve Christ, and to do his work. The Holy Spirit is the down payment of the full gift of God that will come to us when Jesus returns; the Spirit serves as a guarantee of our future inheritance in Christ.

Repenting from sin and clinging to Christ by faith is changing allegiance from the kingdom of Satan to the Kingdom of God. When you do so, you literally are connected with all who have believed God by faith and are rescued from the wrath to come. Water *baptism**, commanded by Jesus for all believers, is an outward sign of this inward work of grace done in us by

. . . .

***baptism** – Baptism is a ritual for believers that involves the application of water on the body in order to represent you being brought into the Body of Christ. It may involve immersion (dunking) in water, poured on the head, or other means of application. Baptism comes from a word "baptidzo" which means "to be placed into." So baptism is important because it is a public demonstration of a spiritual reality; it shows that you have now been placed into Christ. Every believer should be baptized because Jesus asked all of us to do so a public demonstration of our allegiance to him.*

the Holy Spirit to connect us to Christ as our Lord and Leader, and to publicly declare our allegiance and commitment to the risen Lord as his follower.

> To acknowledge Jesus as Savior and Lord is to join an army. Whether you know it or not, you have enlisted.
>
> ~ John White. *The Fight.*
> Downers Grove, IL: InterVarsity Press, 1976, p. 217.

The Enlistment We Make
Lesson 2 Bible Study

Read the following Scriptures and answer briefly the questions associated with each biblical teaching.

1. *The Word becomes flesh, and offers believers eternal salvation.* Read John 1.10-14.

    a. According to John who was this Word, and what is his relationship to God?

    b. What was this Word's relationship to John the Baptizer? What is his relationship to the world?

    c. How does God give people the right to be children of God?

    d. How do we become children of God? (choose the best answer):
        i. Born of blood, or natural descent
        ii. Born by human will, or husband's decision
        iii. Born of God

2. *Salvation from sin and death is given to us by the grace of God, through faith.* Read Ephesians 2.1-10.

    a. How does the *apostle** describe human beings and their relationship to the devil (the "prince of the power of the air"), before they repent and believe in Christ?

    b. List three things that were true of you before God saved you by his mercy.
       i.

       ii.

       iii.

    c. How are we saved? (Choose the best answer):
       i. By grace through faith (as a gift of God)
       ii. By your good works (so you can boast)

    d. For what purpose were we saved – what does God want us to be and do, now that we're saved?

3. *Jesus is the One who defeated the devil in order to liberate and restore creation and humankind.* Read Luke 11.14-23

    a. What did Jesus' enemies accuse him of, after he cast a demon out of a mute man?

    b. In reply, what did Jesus suggest about the nature of a kingdom that is divided against itself?

. . . .

*apostle – Apostle means "one who is sent." This term is used in two ways in the Bible. Most often, as in this case, it refers to people that Jesus personally sent to carry out his work, including the 12 who accompanied him in his earthly ministry, and a person like Paul who received a personal assignment from Jesus in Acts 9. The apostles' eyewitness account is vital to us because their testimony forms everything we know about Christ (see 1 John 1.1-4 and 2 Peter 1.16-18). This is why the Nicene Creed talks about our faith as being "apostolic;" we base our interpretation of the Bible and human history on what the apostles say. The second way the word "apostle" is used (e.g. Eph. 4.11) is in reference to those gifted by the Spirit to be sent with a specific task or mission. Today we call them "missionaries," i.e. people sent out for a specific purpose such as planting churches.

c. What did Jesus say had happened if he cast out demons by the "finger of God" (i.e., the Holy Spirit of God)?

d. How did Jesus describe his power to overcome the "strong man" (the devil) in this parable?

e. Jesus' parable in Luke 11 can be clearly explained in 1 John 3.8. For what reason did Jesus appear on earth?

4. *Jesus of Nazareth has been given absolute authority from the Father to judge and to save.* Read John 5.19-27.

a. How does Jesus explain the works that he does in relationship to what the Father does?

b. If people fail to honor Christ, what does this mean in their relationship to the Father?

c. What did Jesus say about those who hear his Word and believe in the One who sent him?

   i. Has _____ life

   ii. Will not _____

   iii. Passed from _____ to life

5. *No human being can be declared righteous on the basis of their good works; we are all made righteous before God by faith in Jesus Christ alone.* Read Romans 3.9-28.

a. List three ways in which human beings are described regarding their moral situation before God:

   i.

   ii.

   iii.

b. List three things Paul says about how we are righteous before God.

i.

ii.

iii.

c. How then are we justified (declared righteous) before God without obedience to the Law?

6. *We are born again to new life by believing in Jesus Christ.* Read John 3.1-21.

a. Why is it needful that one be born again in order to enter the Kingdom of God?

b. Jesus referred to an Old Testament story in Numbers chapter 21 to help Nicodemus understand how Jesus would die for the sake of humankind on the cross. What symbol was mentioned in the story, and what did the people need to do to be healed? How did Jesus use the story in teaching Nicodemus (cf. v. 15)?

c. Fill in the blanks. (vv. 15-16)

i. The Son of Man must be lifted up so_____
_____.

ii. God so loved the world that he gave his only Son that_____
_____.

iii. God did not send his Son to _____ the world but in order that the world might be _____.

7. *Although once foolish and disobedient, we have now by faith become God's very own children through the grace of God in Jesus.* Read Titus 3.1-8.

   a. How are we as new believers in Christ to relate to

      i. Rulers and authorities

      ii. To all people

   b. Describe the way we were before we repented and believed in Christ.

   c. What happens to us when the "goodness and loving kindness of our God" appeared to us?

   d. How now should we live, having been saved by God's grace?

8. After we believe, the Holy Spirit indwells our bodies and seals us for the Lord's own possession – and for the battle we fight!

   a. Read Ephesians 1.13-14. Fill in the blanks:

      i. When you believed in him, you were sealed by the

         _____.

      ii. The Holy Spirit is a guarantee of our _____ until we acquire possession of it.

   b. Read Romans 8.12-17. Answer the following questions, true or false.

      i. Now that we are indwelt by the Holy Spirit, we don't have to give in to sin.

      ii. We have been adopted by the Spirit's work into God's family.

      iii. We are heirs of God and fellow heirs with Christ, if we suffer with him.

9. *God has called messengers to declare to the world Christ's victory over the devil and sin.* Read Acts 26.12-18. Fill in the blanks. When Paul received a vision from Jesus, what did Jesus appoint him to do?

   a. Be a servant and _____ of the things you will see (v. 16).

   b. Open the eyes of people so they may turn from _____ to light, from the power of _____ to God, that they may receive _____ of sins, and a place among those who are sanctified by _____ (v. 18).

Summary

Everyone who turns to God from their sins (repentance) and believes in Jesus Christ as risen Lord (faith) are saved – forgiven, made whole, and accepted in the Lord's family, by his grace and loving kindness. This invitation to become God's own child involves changing our allegiance from this world and its sin to Christ and his Kingdom. To believe is to turn to God from this world, to swear allegiance to another Master, a new Kingdom, and a new life. Jesus came to destroy the works of the devil, to restore humankind to right relationship with God, and soon, to restore all things in the universe under the reign of God in his Kingdom.

God saves us by his grace, and not because of our obedience to his Law, or our own merit, or good works. We are restored to right relationship to God only by his mercy, on account of Christ's substitutionary ("in our place") death. Now that we are saved, we are enlisted in the fight against sin, evil, and the kingdom of darkness. Truly, the invitation to be saved is a call to join the Lord's beloved army, and to do battle against the world, our old sin nature, and the devil.

After we believe, God seals us with his Holy Spirit who makes his home in us, and gives us the strength, direction, and ability to honor God, serve Christ, and to do his work. The Holy Spirit is the down payment of the full gift of God that will come to us when Jesus returns; the Spirit serves as a guarantee of our future inheritance in Christ. God's gracious benefits are made real by the Holy Spirit: forgiveness of sin, rescue from the devil and the kingdom of darkness, and power to obey the will of God as we live the Christian life.

We cooperate with the Holy Spirit by affirming the truth of the Word of God, by changing our self-talk from negative, destructive, and untrue statements to accurate, statements, consistent with Scripture. We are new creations in Christ, and now we must accept what the authors of the

Bible say in Scripture as the truth about ourselves, our pasts, and most importantly, about our potential and our future. We are not subjects of the kingdom of darkness anymore; we have been brought into the Kingdom of God's Son, the kingdom of the light. Let the redeemed of the Lord begin to say so (Ps. 107.1-3)!

Appendices

The Appendices you should study and meditate upon relevant to this lesson are the following:

Jesus of Nazareth: The Presence of the Future (App. 4)
The Story of God: Our Sacred Roots (App. 5)
From Before to Beyond Time (App. 6)
The Shadow and the Substance (App. 7)

Key Principle

For those who received Him He gave the right to be children of God (John 1.12).

Case Studies

Read and reflect upon the following cases and concepts, and provide answers and insights into their resolution, based on the texts you studied above.

1. **"I don't feel very victorious right now."** Many (if not most) new Christians start off on their Christian journeys with much joy and confidence, only to meet opposition early, and then find themselves struggling with sin and shame. Having started strong, they are both shocked and discouraged that the Christian life is "not as easy as the preacher promised." They still are tempted, they still get angry, they still give in to sin, and they still have to struggle with lust, greed, and pride. They ask themselves, "Where is the victory spoken about in the Bible? Why can't I just call on the Lord and things be made right just at that moment? If God is on my side, why then do I still struggle?" What would you say to someone who felt disillusioned about the Christ Way – who did not feel particularly victorious in the midst of the struggle and stress of everyday life?

2. **"How can I know for sure I really have been forgiven?"** Every growing or immature Christian will encounter doubts about whether they have in fact been saved. Though they have turned their lives over to the Lord, they will inevitably think, say, and do things that are out of sync with their new life in Christ. Sometimes these kind of "speed bumps" in the road cause them to even doubt if they are saved at all. Filled with both doubt and fear, they easily can be persuaded or tempted to ask the

Lord repeatedly to save them again and again. They not only lack all assurance that their first confession of Christ "took," but they also wonder if the whole thing was made up in their minds in the first place. How does your study of the biblical texts above help you resolve this kind of gnawing, ongoing doubt? How do they help a new believer know that they are saved, in spite of how they might feel on any given day (see 1 John 5.11-13)?

3. **"It's amazing. Now that I'm saved by grace, I can do whatever I want. I'm free!"** On one occasion, a new believer was exposed to what the Bible said about grace, Christ's righteousness, and eternal life. Rather than making him humble and grateful, he mistakenly twisted his knowledge into prideful arrogance. He began sharing with his friends, "Since God loves us and saves us by his grace, we don't have to worry about how we live. Whatever we do, he will forgive us, and accept us, not on the basis of what we do, but because of what Jesus did!" How is this new brother in Christ misunderstanding how we should live, now that we have been saved by Christ? What is the true understanding of how we should now live?

Connection

One of the first and most meaningful things that a believer can and must do in beginning their journey into the Story of God is to realize that they are now combatants in the greatest cosmic fight of all time. Honestly, no thunder rolled when we accepted Christ (at least, not normally!) Everything can seem as it was. The truth is, though, everything has changed. We have been rescued from the kingdom of darkness, forgiven of all our transgression, adopted into God's family, and enlisted into God's fighting force for the Kingdom! We are brand new creations in Christ; the old has passed away and the new has come (2 Cor. 5.17).

Determine right now to adopt a fighting spirit, to depend on the Holy Spirit for strength, to pray to the Lord for help each day as you walk with Christ, and to stand your ground in the battles for your mind, your heart, and your soul. God has promised to give you the victory (1 Cor. 15.57), because greater is he that is in you than he that is in the world (1 John 4.4). You now belong to the Lord, and you do not have to identify with your old life with its insecurities, lies, and deceptions. You are a new child of God in Christ, and you must deliberately start to act, talk, and think like that new person. Be patient with yourself; it will take patience and time to learn God's new ways, and to become the new person that he wants you to be.

Ask God for help to live into this new identity, this new self that God has made, set free from the deceitful lusts of the past, renewed in the spirit of your mind, and now liberated to live as a new person with a different nature, a new family, and a new Lord to lead and guide you (Eph. 4.20-24). He has enlisted you into his army, and outfitted you for your journey ahead. So, dear disciple of Jesus, welcome to the family, and welcome to the war!

If you have not been baptized, talk with your Bible study leader, Christian friend, or pastor about your desire and need to be baptized. Be open to following your local church's process to be prepared to be baptized, and follow through as soon as possible. Christ commanded all who believe to be baptized, a sign of our union with him and a public declaration of our allegiance to Jesus and his Kingdom (Mark. 16.14-16; Matt. 28.18-20). Don't wait; Baptism is an outward sign of God's inward grace given to you through the finished work of Jesus on the Cross. Obey him, and be baptized soon!

Affirmation

By faith I have responded to God's forgiving grace, making me a blameless child of God, rescued from the dominion of darkness into the kingdom of the Son.

Prayer

The Te Deum Laudamus is a prayer that has been recited by Christians since the fourth century. It is attributed to Bishop Nicetas of Dacia, c. 335-414, but legend ascribes it to a spontaneous proclamation of Ambrose when he baptized Augustine.

You Are God (Te Deum Laudamus)

You are God: we praise you;
You are the Lord; we acclaim you;
You are the eternal Father: All creation worships you.
To you all angels, all the powers of heaven,
    cherubim and seraphim, sing in endless praise:
Holy, holy, holy Lord, God of power and might,
    heaven and earth are full of your glory.

The glorious company of apostles praise you.
The noble fellowship of prophets praise you.
The white-robed army of martyrs praise you.
Throughout the world the holy church acclaims you;
    Father, of majesty unbounded, your true and only Son,
    worthy of all worship, and the Holy Spirit, advocate and guide.

You, Christ, are the king of glory, the eternal Son of the Father.
When you became man to set us free you did not shun the virgin's womb.
You overcame the sting of death and opened the kingdom of heaven
    to all believers.
You are seated at God's right hand in glory.
We believe that you will come and be our judge.
Come then, Lord and help your people,
    bought with the price of your own blood,
    and bring us with your saints to glory everlasting.

Heart Cry to the Lord

Eternal Father, my maker and Father of my Lord Jesus Christ, thank you so much for being so gracious to us in sending Jesus down to save us. We did not deserve your love or your forgiveness, but still, you cared for us, sent him to show us the way, and offered him up in our place as a sacrifice for sin. You have sealed us with the Holy Spirit, adopted us into your family, and freed us from the fear of death and eternal punishment. Now, what should I offer you in the light of such love and mercy? I give you my heart, my life, my money and time, and all my relationships. While I know it will undoubtedly take me time to get to know you, I want you to know that I am ready for a new life, a new direction, and a new journey. Make me a part of your great Story, O God, and lead me by the Spirit you have given me. I will honor you in what I do, as you help me. In Jesus' name I pray, amen.

For More Study

At www.tumi.org/sacredroots, we have a section dedicated to additional written and video resources.

Robert Webber. *Who Gets to Narrate the World*. Downers Grove, IL: InterVarsity Press, 2008.

For the Next Session

In the next session, you will explore *The Entrance We Get* including these topics:
1. By being "in Christ" we receive and experience all he is and does.
2. We participate through our membership in the household of God, built on the apostles and prophets.
3. Each local church serves as an agent of the Kingdom.

Scripture Memory

Romans 10.9-10

Assignments

1. If you have not been baptized, meet with your pastor and ask to be baptized.
2. Pray daily for three friends who need to enlist in the Lord's army and be saved. Look for God to give you opportunities to share your faith with them.
3. Start writing in a notebook or journal, listing insights you receive and questions you want to ask a mature believer in your church.

THE ENTRANCE WE GET
Linking Our Life with the Life of God in Christ

> So then you are no longer strangers and aliens, but you are fellow citizens with the saints and members of the household of God, built on the foundation of the apostles and prophets, Christ Jesus himself being the cornerstone, in whom the whole structure, being joined together, grows into a holy temple in the Lord. In him you also are being built together into a dwelling place for God by the Spirit.
>
> ~ Ephesians 2.19-22

Objectives

By the end of this session, you should embrace the *Entrance We Get* by:

- Believing we are joined to Jesus by faith (i.e., we are now "in Christ"), we receive and experience all that he is, provides, and does.
- Believing that through the Spirit's working, we now possess membership in the household of God, whose cornerstone is Jesus Christ, and whose foundation is the apostles and prophets.
- Believing that each local church is an embassy of the Kingdom of God, representing the interests and intentions of heaven itself, with believers serving as ambassadors and agents of that Kingdom.

Opening Prayer for Wisdom

Eternal God, my Father, you say in your Word that you are the source of all knowledge and wisdom. I acknowledge this as the truth, dear Father, and I ask that you impart into me divine wisdom, that I may be able to rightly divide the Word of truth (2 Timothy 2.15). Please instruct and teach me in the way I should go (Psalm 32.8), and direct my steps. Incline my ear to hear your voice, and correct me now in the way I think and speak, and lead me when I have gone astray.

Father, grant me the gift of discernment, and enable me as I study to know the difference between godly and ungodly teachings, spirits, and gifts. Show me by the Holy Spirit what your will is, and give me insight into how I can carry out your intentions with my whole heart.

Dear Lord, please help me to be quick to hear and listen, slow to speak, and slow to anger (James 1.19). Let the words of my mouth and the thoughts of my heart be acceptable in your sight. Allow me to speak your truth with wisdom in order that all with whom I speak may understand and benefit by your truth.

Teach me now in this study as I receive your Word and instruction. I ask for these things in the strong name of Jesus, my Lord and Savior, Amen.

Contact

1. **"Why is there such a difference between what my condition is and what the Bible says my position before God is?"** Many new Christians experience a wide gap between what the Scriptures declare regarding their status before God (e.g., as forgiven, as reconciled, as adopted children, as chosen by God), and the way things go in their lives day by day (bouts of doubt, worry, frustration, self-condemnation, and fear). It nearly seems as if the two visions of the Christian life (what the Bible says versus how I feel day by day) are incompatible and contradict one another. As we live out our Christian lives day by day, how should we understand this tension between what the Scriptures say about who we are in Christ versus how we feel about ourselves?

2. **"When will I start acting like the person the Bible says I am?"** A large part of being an effective disciple of Christ is resolving the conflict internally between *who we used to be before we met Christ* and *who we are now that we have believed*. Oftentimes, who we used to be seems to be a stronger, more realistic, and more authentic view of ourselves than what the Bible or our teachers and pastors say about us. How can a new Christian identify with the texts and declarations of the Bible even when it appears that who we used to be is our more "natural" self, the "me" we feel most comfortable with, and seems to be most true about us?

3. **"I'll just stay home and walk with the Lord by myself."** On one occasion a new adult believer who had recently come out of the drug culture accepted Christ, and began his journey of living a new life in Christ. The problem, however, is that he felt dramatically awkward in the presence of other Christians, largely because of the lifestyle that he had lived so long on the streets – harming his body, his family, and his relationships with others. Frustrated and exhausted, one day he exclaimed, "That's it! I just don't think I can live my Christian life with the people at church. They are good people and all, but they just can't get where I'm coming from right now. I think I want to keep walking with Christ, but I'll just stay at home, and I'll walk with the Lord by

myself." What would you say to him about his decision – is it a good one, and if not, why not?

Content

In the last session (*The Enlistment We Make*) we learned that when we turned to God from idols and sin (repentance) and believed in Jesus of Nazareth as the risen Lord (faith), we simultaneously made a decision to enlist in the Lord's army, by turning away from the kingdom of Satan to the Kingdom of God's own Son.

Now we will explore the riches we have since, through faith, we have been joined to Christ, and are said to be "in Christ." Our union with Jesus by faith provides us with a new status and relationship before God (our position), a position of favor, adoption, and blessing as his child and citizen of his Kingdom. In addition to this, being "in Christ" also enables us to walk in his victory day by day as we fight the good fight of faith – and receive the power to walk in the Holy Spirit (our condition)!

According to the New Testament, every one who believes in Jesus has been baptized into (joined with) Christ by the working of the Holy Spirit (cf. 1 Corinthians 12.13 "For in one Spirit we were all baptized into one body – Jews or Greeks, slaves or free – and all were made to drink of one Spirit.") When the Spirit baptized (placed us) into Christ, we were not only rescued from God's wrath and given an eternity full of joy in his presence, but we also received a new status and relationship with God, given specifically to us because we have now been made one with Christ (see "33 Blessings in Christ" in the appendix).

Truly, we have been blessed with many blessings because we trusted in Christ for our salvation. Our sins have been forgiven (Eph. 1.7; Col. 1.13), we have been reconciled to God, restored to fellowship with him (2 Cor. 6.18-19), and we have been adopted as a new child into the Father's own household (Rom. 8.14-15, 23). One of the many wonderful benefits we have in Christ is our new membership and place in the Church, the Body of Christ. By faith, we have been joined to all believers everywhere, connected to God and to each other, and given the privilege to trust and grow and serve the Kingdom together as one people.

Thank God, we need never fight the good fight as isolated people, in our own strength, by ourselves alone. All believers, from those who first believed until now, make up the one, amazing, Body of Christ. While there are many assemblies and local churches (church with a small "c"), there is in fact only one Church which began with Jesus and the apostles, and has been set apart for God's purposes (church with a capital "C"). The Nicene Creed declares that this church is one, holy, apostolic, and *catholic** (universal), and is made up of many local churches around the world, all throughout history.

Truly, then, let us listen to the apostle Paul's good word to the Philippians and apply it to our own walk in Christ:

> But our citizenship is in heaven, and from it we await a Savior, the Lord Jesus Christ, who will transform our lowly body to be like his glorious body, by the power that enables him even to subject all things to himself.
>
> ~ Phlippians 3.20-21

Indeed, every believer is a heavenly citizen, and every local church is an embassy of the Kingdom of God where we gather for teaching, for worship, for spiritual formation, and for service to Christ with other believers. In the early years of the Church, the Holy Spirit led Christ's people to lay out precisely what we believe, how we are to worship, and what the Scriptures would be. These core beliefs undergird the faith for all believers, everywhere, and is called the Great Tradition. This represents that teaching and practice which the apostles taught, written in the Bible, summarized in the great creeds and councils of the Church, and defended by the believers throughout history (see *Going Forward by Looking Back* and *The Nicene Creed* in the Appendix).

> Every time the Church assembles . . . it proclaims also the end of the world and the failure of the world. It contradicts the world's claim to provide men with a valid justification for their existence, it renounces the world; it affirms, since it is made up of the baptized, that it is only on the other side of death to this world that life can assume its meaning . . . Christian worship is the strongest denial that can be hurled in the face of the world's claim to provide men with an effective and sufficient justification of their life. There is no more emphatic protest against the pride and the despair of the world than that implied in Church worship."
>
> ~ Jean-Jacques von Allmen. *Worship: Its Theology and Practice.* London: Lutterworth, 1966, p. 63.

. . . .

***catholic** – Catholic does not mean the Roman Catholic Church, but means "universal", referring to all Christians throughout time, from every tribe, language, people, and nation. In the Apostles' and Nicene Creeds, the term catholic refers to the Church's universality, through all ages and times, of all languages and peoples it refers to no particular tradition or denominational express (e.g. as in Roman Catholic).

The Entrance We Get
Lesson 3 Bible Study
Read the following Scriptures and answer briefly the questions associated with each biblical teaching.

1. *Through the resurrection of Jesus, God has granted to us a living hope, and the promise of eternal life.* Read 1 Peter 1.3-12.

   a. List at least three blessings you have in Christ.

      i.

      ii.

      iii.

   b. What are the results when we suffer grief in trials? (v. 6-7)

   c. Even though we do not see the Lord physically present among us now, how do we still understand our salvation in him? (vv. 8-12)

2. *Jesus is the Living Stone, and we who believe are the chosen people of God.* Read 1 Peter 2.4-10.

   a. Since we are a holy priesthood in Christ, what work has God given us to do? (v. 4-5)

   b. List four things that are true of us, the people of God.

      i.

      ii.

      iii.

      iv.

3. *Through our trust in Christ, and our baptism into him, we have been joined with Jesus – in his death, burial, resurrection – and now, in his new life.*

a. Read Romans 6.3-10. List three things that happened to us when we were baptized into Christ.

i.

ii.

iii.

b. Since we died with Christ, and likewise rose with him from the dead (by faith), what strength does sin now have over us? (vv. 9-10)

c. How are we to count ourselves in connection to sin and its power over us today? (vv. 11-13)

4. *Jesus is the center of the Christian life, the one we must continue to follow in all things.* Read Colossians 2.1-10.

a. Why does Paul describe Christ as "the mystery of God," the one in whom is found all the treasures of wisdom and knowledge? (v. 3-4)

b. How does Paul challenge the Colossians to respond to Christ, now that they have received him as their Savior and Lord? (v. 6-7)

c. What should believers always be on guard against? (v. 8).

d. How does v. 10 describe Jesus' nature, both as God and man?

5. *The believer is blessed with abundant favor and blessings "in Christ."* Read Ephesians 1.3-14.

a. List at least five blessings you have received as a result of being "in Christ."

i.

ii.

    iii.

    iv.

    v.

  b. What did the Holy Spirit do to us after we believed in Christ (v. 13-14)? How does the gift of the Spirit relate to the blessings that are to come to us?

6. *We who were once far away from God have been brought near to him through Christ.* Read Ephesians 2.13-22.

  a. How did Christ make peace between believers who are of a different racial, ethnic, and cultural background? (vv. 13-18)

  b. Read Ephesians 2.18-22. Match the group with the truth about them:

i. Fellow citizens with the saints	___Building a dwelling place for God
ii. Apostles and prophets	___The foundation is built on them
iii. Jesus	___No longer foreigners and aliens
iv. The Spirit	___The chief cornerstone

7. *God has chosen to reveal the glories of his grace through his people, the Church.* Read Ephesians 3.8-11. Fill in the blanks: God, who created all things, through the _____ revealed the manifold _____ of God, made known to the _____ in heavenly places.

8. *In past ages and times, God did not reveal to humankind his great mystery that is now being revealed to all people through the apostles' testimony about Christ and even non-Jewish believers!*

a. Read Colossians 1.24-29. Choose the best answer. What is the mystery that Paul said was kept hidden for ages but now revealed to us?

   i. The day and hour of Jesus' return

   ii. Christ in us, the hope of glory

   iii. The kind of death Paul would experience

b. Why do you think the news that Christ among the Gentiles (non-Jews) is viewed as such a great revelation among the believers of Paul's time?

Summary

The apostles in the New Testament testify that every believer in Christ has been joined to him and his work, by the baptizing power of the Holy Spirit. The Holy Spirit has placed us into Christ, linking us with his death, burial, resurrection, and new life. In Jesus, we are no longer objects of God's wrath, and have no fear of being punished for the many transgressions (breaking of God's commandments) which we have committed. God has provided us in Jesus with an entirely new status and relationship with himself, and has blessed us with numerous, wonderful, and gracious benefits and blessings in Christ.

Of the many wonderful gifts we have received, one of the most significant is our new membership and place in the Church, the Body of Christ. God has joined us all in Christ, and therefore, now, to all other believers, and granted us both the privilege and responsibility to live and grow together as God's family (1 John 3.1-3), as Christ's body (Rom. 12.4-8), and as a temple of the Holy Spirit (1 Cor. 3.16-17). We were never designed to live our Christian lives in isolation, just as a human body cannot function effectively with only feet or only hands. No, all the members are important in order that the body might grow and mature, and fulfill the work it was meant to accomplish.

As such every believer is to view himself/herself as a heavenly citizen, one who is joined to Christ and to the living hope of his return to earth. In this vein, every local church can be understood as an embassy of the Kingdom of God, an outpost of the heavenly realm, where believers gather to grow, worship, and serve the Lord with other growing Christians. From the beginning, the Holy Spirit has led Christ's people to identify, confess, and defend the core teachings and practices of the apostles, as laid out in the Bible and taught through the years by the Church. This Great Tradition, this core theology and practice of the Church, is believed, preached, and celebrated in local churches around the world, wherever Christ is acknowledged to be both Lord and Christ.

The entrance we get, immediately after we believe, is membership in the Church, a membership that can only be fleshed out in a local church with pastor and real people, where we can grow, worship, and serve Christ together.

Appendices

The Appendices you should study and meditate upon relevant to this lesson are the following:

Thirty-three Blessings in Christ (App. 14)
In Christ (App. 8)
Jesus of Nazareth: The Presence of the Future (App. 4)
Going Forward by Looking Back: Toward an Evangelical Retrieval of the Great Tradition (App. 16)
The Nicene Creed (App. 24 and 25)
The Apostles' Creed (App. 26)

Key Principle

In Christ we have received every spiritual blessing (Ephesians 1.3).

Case Studies

Read and reflect upon the following cases and concepts, and provide answers and insights into their resolution, based on the texts you studied above.

1. **"I don't need to get baptized, do I? I already did it once."** A sister who recently accepted Christ was discussing with her pastor whether she needed to be baptized, since she had already been baptized as a child. Of course, when she was baptized so many years ago, she neither understood nor committed herself to Christ – she was only 12 years old, had no clue what baptism was about, and now was pretty sure that she had not believed in Christ when she did it. What would you advise for that new adult believer – should she seek to be baptized again, but this time, to do it with the full knowledge of what it means, and with a clear sense of her own faith and commitment to Jesus Christ as Lord and Savior?

2. **My friend says I should "name it and claim it" to receive God's blessings. How does that jive with what the Bible says?"** A new believer is attending a church where Christians are encouraged to "name and claim" the blessings of God for life, for physical needs, for

healing in sickness, and for favor in the midst of trouble. A lot of the focus is on physical blessings (money, health, and possessions), and little attention is made of our spiritual blessings "in Christ." How should we understand the relationship between God's declaration that we have received all spiritual blessings in Christ (e.g., Eph. 1.3), and the widespread emphasis in many churches on claiming God's blessings and favor in the physical things of life (i.e., "health and wealth" issues). How do we properly understand the emphasis between these two domains of God's blessing and care?

3. **I can't get what I need from one, local church alone. I get what I need from different churches around town – worship from church A, teaching from church B, and fellowship from church C.** Is that okay? "Church-hopping" is a common occurrence among many followers of Christ today. Convinced that they simply cannot get all they need to grow and thrive in a single local church, many Christians have taken it upon themselves to "church hop," attending different churches at different times to access different teaching, programs, or worship opportunities. In a world where everyone is accustomed to "getting what they need" from different sources, believers have applied the same logic to church attendance. This is usually built on the notion that no one church could possibly meet all the needs of the average Christian or Christian family. Those who embrace this argue that they get the best possible experience by worshiping with one congregation, listening to the sermon at another congregation, and fellowshipping in small group with another. If a healthy local church is an embassy of the Kingdom, why might it not be best to engage in "church hopping" our way to Christian maturity?

Connection

Spend time this week reviewing the texts that speak of the blessings and benefits you now have as a baptized believer in Christ. You can neither reflect upon nor claim these many blessings if you have no knowledge of what they are, and what they mean for your Christian life! Study the verses in the Appendix "33 Blessings in Christ" and become familiar with these truths. The more you understand what God has given to you, the better you will able to make them a part of your own internal self talk, and part of your prayer language as you give thanks and make requests to the Lord.

If you have not yet joined a local church (I mean, embassy of the Kingdom of God!), then ask the Lord to guide you in the days and weeks ahead to come to the place (not places!) he would have you attend. You need to be under a good pastor's authority, to fellowship with other committed Christians, and to find avenues where you can use your gifts to serve and edify others. The key is making a commitment to not only attend an assembly, but to enquire into what it means to become a member, a living part of the body where you gather with others. Don't be discouraged if it seems awkward or lonely at the beginning; persevere in your participation, and trust the Lord to open doors of friendship and service as you go. God will lead you, and if you have patience, you will bear much fruit (Gal. 6.7-9).

Affirmation

Because I am baptized into Christ, I share all the blessings, glory, hope, and sufferings of Christ with all Christians everywhere and throughout time.

Prayer

Billy Sunday, who was a popular National League Baseball player in the 1880's became a celebrated and influential evangelist in the first two decades of the 20th century. Sunday's preaching attracted large crowds to his campaigns in some of America's largest cities. In one of his famous sermons exalting the all sufficiency of Jesus Christ, Billy Sunday paid tribute to the Savior with these words.*

* Some sources say "Author unknown," one website says it is attributed to St. Patrick, but a few say Billy Sunday.

Christ My All

Christ for sickness, Christ for health,
Christ for poverty, Christ for wealth,
Christ for joy, Christ for sorrow,
Christ today, and Christ tomorrow;

Christ my Life and Christ my Light,
Christ for morning, noon and night;
Christ when all around gives way,
Christ my Everlasting Stay;

Christ my Rest, Christ my Food,
Christ above my Highest Good;
Christ my Well Beloved, my Friend,
Christ my Pleasure, without end;

Christ my Savior, Christ my Lord,
Christ my Portion, Christ my God;
Christ my Shepherd, I His sheep,
Christ Himself my soul doth keep;

Christ my Leader, Christ my Peace,
Christ hath brought my soul's release;
Christ my Righteousness divine,
Christ for me, for He is mine;

Christ my Wisdom, Christ my Meat,
Christ restores my wand'ring feet;
Christ my Advocate and Priest,
Christ who ne'er forgets the least;

Christ my Teacher, Christ my Guide,
Christ my Rock, in Christ I hide;
Christ the everlasting Bread,
Christ his precious blood hath shed;

Christ hath brought us near to God,
Christ the everlasting Word;
Christ my Master, Christ my Head,
Christ Who for my sins hath bled;

Christ my Glory, Christ my Crown,
Christ the Plant of great Renown;
Christ my Comforter on high,
Christ my Hope draws ever nigh.

~ H.W.S. *The Speakers Quote Book:*
Over 4,500 Illustrations and Quotations for All Occasions.
Roy B.Zuck, Grand Rapids, MI: Kregel Publications, 1997, p. 57.

**Heart Cry
to the Lord**

Eternal God, God and Father of my Lord Jesus Christ, thank you for making me one with your Son. Thank you so much, Lord, for the many wonderful gifts and blessings I have received through Christ, and thank you especially for the great blessing of making me a member of your people, your Church, and the Body of Christ. By faith, you have made me one with all other believers, and granted to me both the honor and duty of living, growing, and serving together in a local church, a living assembly revealed as your family, as the body of Jesus, and as the temple of the Holy Spirit. To know you is to love your people, for you are love.

I know that you did not intend for me to live my Christian life as a maverick, to try to fight the good fight by myself, alone and in isolation. Lead me to the local church where you want me to grow, under a pastor who can keep watch over my soul, and with Christians I can love – those fellow warriors with whom I can use my gifts to build up as we testify of your love to our neighbors. Thank you for your church. Make me a fruitful and kind member of your people, and help me to grow as I fellowship among them, for Christ's sake, amen.

For More Study

At www.tumi.org/sacredroots, we have a section dedicated to additional written and video resources.

John Eldridge. *Epic: The Story God Is Telling.* Thomas Nelson, Inc., Nashville, TN: 2004.

For the Next Session

In the next session, you will explore ***The Endowment We Receive*** including these topics:
1. The Holy Spirit endows each believer with gifts to serve the Body.
2. We are given freedom in Christ to practice our gifts.
3. We receive power to grow together in maturity and unity.

Scripture Memory

Ephesians 1.3

Assignments

1. Write a poem or letter to the Lord, thanking him for all he has done.
2. Read the Nicene Creed in the Appendix. In your journal, summarize the key truths the Nicene Creed tells us about the army you have enlisted in.
3. Meet with a mature believer in the church and ask how the church has helped him/her live the Christian life that would have been impossible to do alone.

THE ENDOWMENT WE RECEIVE
The Holy Spirit's Role in the Good Fight of Faith

> And he gave the apostles, the prophets, the *evangelists**, the *pastors** and teachers, to equip the saints for the work of ministry, for building up the body of Christ, until we all attain to the unity of the faith and of the knowledge of the Son of God, to mature manhood, to the measure of the stature of the fullness of Christ, so that we may no longer be children, tossed to and fro by the waves and carried about by every wind of doctrine, by human cunning, by craftiness in deceitful schemes. Rather, speaking the truth in love, we are to grow up in every way into him who is the head, into Christ.
>
> ~ Ephesians 4.11-15

Objectives

By the end of this session, you should embrace the *Endowment We Receive* by believing that:

- The Holy Spirit indwells every believer, and endows each believer with gifts to serve the Body.
- We are given freedom in Christ to practice our gifts, as the Holy Spirit provides us opportunities to serve.
- Through the Spirit's direction, gifts, and strength, we are provided with sufficient power to live in strong fellowship with other believers in the church, growing together in maturity and unity.

Opening Prayer for Wisdom

Eternal God, my Father, you say in your Word that you are the source of all knowledge and wisdom. I acknowledge this as the truth, dear Father, and I ask that you impart into me divine wisdom, that I may be able to rightly divide the Word of truth (2 Timothy 2.15). Please instruct and teach me in

- -

*Evangelists refers to those workers gifted by the Spirit to effectively communicate the good news of the Gospel to the lost. While all believers are commanded to share the gospel, some are more gifted in this area and helpful for building up the body of Christ.

*Pastors are "shepherds" assigned to care for the flock, i.e. the local church. Pastors must protect the flock through their Bible teaching, godly counsel and encouragement, warning the sheep against dangers, and leading the flock to carry out the work of God in their communities.

the way I should go (Psalm 32.8), and direct my steps. Incline my ear to hear your voice, and correct me now in the way I think and speak, and lead me when I have gone astray.

Father, grant me the gift of discernment, and enable me as I study to know the difference between godly and ungodly teachings, spirits, and gifts. Show me by the Holy Spirit what your will is, and give me insight into how I can carry out your intentions with my whole heart.

Dear Lord, please help me to be quick to hear and listen, slow to speak, and slow to anger (James 1.19). Let the words of my mouth and the thoughts of my heart be acceptable in your sight. Allow me to speak your truth with wisdom in order that all with whom I speak may understand and benefit by your truth.

Teach me now in this study as I receive your Word and instruction. I ask for these things in the strong name of Jesus, my Lord and Savior, Amen.

Contact

1. **"Are the apostles and other key leaders all gone now?"** In a Bible study on the book of Ephesians, a new Christian read Ephesians 4.11-15 and asked the question, "I thought that the apostles, prophets, and people like that don't exist now in the church. What does this text mean? Do we have people who function as apostles and prophets today, and, if so, where are they? If I understand what Paul is saying, God gave us these folk so that they could help us learn how to minister to other people. That is really cool!" What do you think the text means for us today – is God continuing to provide gifted leaders to the Church so that Christians can become effective ministers in the world?

2. **"I don't even know my pastor."** In a men's prayer meeting, the subject came up about the need for us to be under a pastor's authority and training. One fellow said that, "Yeah, God has provided us with pastors in order that they might shield and protect us from falsehood and spiritual dangers. They are God's shepherds, given authority from the Lord to help us as Christ's sheep, that we might be well fed, strong, and ready to do ministry." One new Christian in the church said, "I hear what you're saying, but honestly, I can't seem to wrap my mind around this. I've only spoken with the pastor once, (which was a long time ago, when I first came to the church), and I don't really know him at all. Honestly, I don't know my pastor. How can he shepherd me if I don't know him?" What advice would you give to this new believer – what do you believe God intends for him to do about his lack of relationship with his pastor?

3. **"How do you really know when you have the Holy Spirit?"** A young Christian was troubled about a conversation she had on the bus with a person who said that they were a "Pentecostal" Christian. This person told her that she needed to get the Holy Spirit, which would be shown by her "baptism in the Holy Spirit," followed by her *speaking in tongues**. The young sister in reply said, "I learned last week in Bible Study that every person who repents and believes in Jesus is sealed with the Holy Spirit, and that he lives within them immediately when they believe. We also learned that he gives us gifts to help us serve other Christians in the body of Christ, and that tongues are one gift of the Spirit – but does every Christian have to have every gift? How does that work?" The sister is now interested in finding out more about the Holy Spirit – how should she proceed to learn?

Content

In the last session (*The Entrance We Get*) we learned that when we believed in Jesus, we were baptized into Christ, and inherited a host of blessings in Christ. Now we will explore some of what the Bible says about the Holy Spirit, his work and blessing in the lives of believers, and see how he provides special gifts and abilities to help us grow and become strong as we walk with the Lord in his Story, fighting the good fight of faith.

The Holy Spirit is the pledge (down payment) of the future inheritance that we as Christians will receive when the Lord Jesus Christ returns to establish his Kingdom. The Spirit gives every believer a spiritual gift in order to edify (build up) other members of the body of Christ in the local church. The Holy Spirit comes to indwell every believer; no one is left out because the Body requires the participation, contribution, and involvement of all members of the body. Through his grace, God also provides us with forgiveness, and freedom from sin, guilt, and condemnation so we can serve others in Christ's name with courage and boldness. He enables us to grow as we reflect upon the Word of God (theology), exalt his name in the Word and through the

. . . .

*Speak in tongues – When the Church was birthed by the coming of the Holy Spirit (Acts 2), believers received gifts from him, including the ability to speak in languages they did not normally know how to speak. This gift is mentioned in the New Testament as available to believers for their upbuilding (1 Cor. 12.1-31), while in other instances new believers were given this same ability to speak in languages they had not learned, upon receiving Christ by faith (e.g. Acts 10.44-46). In some churches today, it is believed that every Christian must follow this pattern of speaking in a language they have never learned, while other churches believe that this is a gift of the Holy Spirit, bestowed on some and not others. Other churches believe that speaking in tongues was only for the early church and that this gift is not given to believers today.

Lord's Supper (worship), be formed spiritually as we walk together in the spiritual disciplines (discipleship), and share the Good News in word and deed (witness).

As we continue to grow in our ability to worship God and fight this fight, we become mature in our faith so we can equip other believers. The more believers grow in maturity, the more unity there is in the church, which is pleasing to Christ.

> The Holy Spirit is God's representative. He mirrors God's truth. That means if you sense the Spirit leading your thoughts or guiding your actions, His guidance always lines up with the truth of God's Word. The Spirit never leads us in ways that oppose Scripture. He won't; He can't. He represents and lifts up the person of Jesus. He gives illumination to the character and ways of God.
>
> So when you believe the Spirit is guiding your life, use this test: Does this match up with the truth of the Bible? If not, send it packing to the island of misfit thoughts. We are all capable of imagination and wandering thoughts. Remember Paul's words of advice to hold those thoughts captive and see if they obey the truth of Christ. If they don't agree with Scripture, they're not from the Spirit – and they don't belong in your thought closet.
>
> ~ Jennifer Rothschild.
> *Self Talk, Soul Talk: What to Say When You Talk to Yourself.*
> Eugene, OR: Harvest House Publishers, 2001, pp. 54-55.

The Endowment We Receive
Lesson 4 Bible Study
Read the following Scriptures and answer briefly the questions associated with each biblical teaching.

1. *Jesus prayed for us, and for all those who would come to believe in him as Lord and Savior.* Read John 17.20-26. List three things that Jesus asks of the Father on our behalf.

   a.

   b.

   c.

2. *The Holy Spirit now indwells (lives inside) every Christian who has repented and believed in Jesus Christ.* Read Romans 8.9-17 and answer the following questions:

   a. Can someone possess salvation in Christ and not have the Holy Spirit? (vv. 9-10)

   b. How will those who believe be raised from the dead? (v. 11)

   c. How do we know those who are in fact the children of God? (vv. 14-15)

   d. How does the Spirit help us know that we belong to God? (vv. 16-17)

3. *God the Father has granted us spiritual gifts of grace through the Holy Spirit for the upbuilding of the one body of Christ.* Read Romans 12.3-8. List some of the gifts of the Holy Spirit that are mentioned in this passage.

   a.

   b.

   c.

   d.

   e.

4. *There are varieties of gifts, services, and activities provided by the Holy Spirit, but he provides each member unique gifts to be used to build up other Christians.* Read 1 Corinthians 12.4-11. Choose the best answer:

   a. Spiritual gifts are given so believers can have good self-esteem.

   b. Spiritual gifts are given for the common good.

   c. Believers can choose which gifts they have.

   d. Some people never receive a spiritual gift.

5. *Believers are to be good stewards of God's wondrous gifts of grace, using them in such a way that the Lord himself might be glorified through Jesus Christ.* Read 1 Peter 4.7-11. Match the phrase with the corresponding truth:

   a. Love each other   ___With the strength God provides

   b. Show hospitality   ___Covers a multitude of sins

   c. Use your gift   ___As though using the words of God

   d. Speak   ___Without grumbling

   e. Serve   ___Serve one another, as stewards of God's grace

6. *The Holy Spirit has called us to be free, both from guilt and condemnation. He grants us power to please God, and not to use our freedom as an excuse to do whatever we want.* Read Galatians 5.13-16. Fill in the blanks.

   a. You were called to _____.

   b. Do not use your freedom as an opportunity _____, but to _____ one another.

7. *We have a choice, to either live by those things the Holy Spirit wants us to do or, by the inclinations of our old sin nature. Either way we choose, the result will be evident in our lives.* Read Galatians 5.16-24, and answer the following questions (true or false):

   a. T or F. If we walk in the Spirit, then we will not gratify the desire of our old nature.

   b. T or F. The Holy Spirit agrees with our old nature about what is right.

   c. T or F. While the works of our old nature are hidden, the fruit of the Spirit is clearly visible.

8. *Christ promised to send the Holy Spirit to equip believers to do his work in the world.* Read John16.5-15. List at least three things that Jesus said the Holy Spirit would do for us.

   a.

   b.

   c.

9. *The believer is called to cooperate in every way with the Holy Spirit, obeying his Word and following his promptings.* Read the following Scriptures and describe how we are to respond to the Holy Spirit.

   a. Romans 8.22-27

   b. Ephesians 4.30

   c. Galatians 5.16

   d. Ephesians 5.18

   e. 1 Thessalonians 5.19

10. *God has provided gifted men and women whose task it is to make Christ's body strong and mature.* Read Ephesians 4.11-15. What specific leaders has the Lord given to the Church in order that it might become fully mature in Christ?

11. *The Holy Spirit gives us the ability to understand spiritual truth and empowers us to be filled with the fulness of God.* Read Ephesians 3.16-19. List three things Paul prays that the Spirit would do in us.

   a.

   b.

   c.

Summary

Jesus prayed for us, and for all those who would come to believe in him as Lord and Savior. He promised that the Holy Spirit would come and make his home in us. Now, the Holy Spirit indwells (lives inside) every Christian who repents and believes in Jesus Christ. He provides each individual Christian with special gifts and abilities designed to build believers up in Christ, to help them grow to maturity in Jesus.

Truly, the Holy Spirit is the pledge (down payment) of the future inheritance that believers will receive when the Lord Jesus Christ returns to establish his Kingdom. God the Father has graciously granted each believer spiritual gifts through the Holy Spirit to strengthen and build up his people. While there may be varieties of gifts, services, and activities provided by the Holy Spirit, he gives each Christian unique gifts to be used to build up other Christians. Every believer has gifts, and each one is called on to use their gifts to make the body of Christ strong and mature.

We are called to be good stewards of these wondrous gifts of God's grace, using them in such a way that the Lord himself might be glorified through Jesus Christ. In the Spirit, we are called to live free, not as slaves to our old nature, but rather as channels of the Spirit, through whom his fruit may be borne. We need only yield to him, and follow him in all things.

Appendices

The Appendices you should study and meditate upon relevant to this lesson are the following:

Our Declaration of Dependence: Freedom in Christ (App. 9)
Jesus of Nazareth: The Presence of the Future (App. 4)

> The same breath is blown into the flute, cornet, and bagpipe, but different music is produced according to the different instruments. In the same way the one Spirit works in us, God's children, but different results are produced, and God is glorified through them according to each one's temperament and personality.
>
> ~ Sadhu Sandar Singh.
> Richard J. Foster and James Bryan Smith, Eds.
> *Devotional Classics: Revised Edition:*
> *Selected Readings for Individuals and Groups.*
> Renovaré, Inc. (HarperCollins Publishers), New York. 1993, p. 291.

Key Principle

It is God who works in you to will and to act according to his good purpose (Philippians 2.13).

Case Studies

Read and reflect upon the following cases and concepts, and provide answers and insights into their resolution, based on the texts you studied above.

1. **Can the Holy Spirit ever leave a Christian?** Every now and then every believer will be faced with the temptation to doubt their salvation, even thinking that the Holy Spirit has left them. Some teachings assert that a person who has repented and believed in Christ can, due to their own deliberate disobedience to God, actually act in such a way as not to be Christ's child anymore. Look up the following Scriptures and answer this question: can the Holy Spirit ever leave a Christian?

   a. 1 John 5.11-13:

   b. Ephesians 1.13-14:

   c. Romans 8.31-39:

2. **How do I know that something is from the Holy Spirit and not me?** One of the main concerns of any growing believer in Jesus is the control of their own thoughts and self-talk. Even though we have been saved and belong to Jesus Christ, the enemy still has access to our thoughts, and can suggest things to us that are neither from the Lord nor for our benefit. Not every thought that pops into your mind is from the Lord! The devil is a liar and a deceiver (John 8.44), and we can overcome him because the Holy Spirit (the One who indwells us) is stronger than he (1 John 4.4)!

   We can imitate our Lord, resisting the devil by understanding the Scriptures, and refuse both to accept or take ownership of all the thoughts and self-talk that may go through our minds (Rom. 12.1-2; 2 Cor. 10.3-5). Read the account of Jesus' temptation by the devil, and notice how he answered the devil's lies with the Word of God, so you can follow his example (Matt. 4.1-11).

3. **What is the relationship of the Holy Spirit to the Word of God?** The safe, powerful way to know the Spirit's mind is to become familiar with his Word. The Bible says that the Holy Spirit carried the authors of the Bible along in such a way that what they wrote was inspired by God himself (2 Pet. 1.20-21; 2 Tim. 3.15-17). As we hear the Bible preached, read it through, memorize verses, study passages, and meditate on its

content, we can come to know the mind of the Holy Spirit. The Christian's offensive weapon to combat lies is the Word of God, the "sword of the Spirit" (Eph. 6.17). Why is it important to weigh all statements we hear against the teachings of the Spirit's sword, the Bible (see 1 Thess. 5.19-21)?

Connection

As a new and growing Christian, it is important that you understand the gift of the Holy Spirit, which every one who believes in Christ receives. "On the last day of the feast, the great day, Jesus stood up and cried out, 'If anyone thirsts, let him come to me and drink. Whoever believes in me, as the Scripture has said, "Out of his heart will flow rivers of living water."' Now this he said about the Spirit, whom those who believed in him were to receive, for as yet the Spirit had not been given, because Jesus was not yet glorified" (John 7.37-39). As a believer, you have been sealed with the Holy Spirit until the day Christ returns and redeems us (Eph. 1.13-14). At the proper time in history, God sent his Son to redeem us in order that we who believe might be adopted into his family as his children. Now, because we are his children, God sent the Spirit of Jesus into our hearts, crying, "Abba! Father!" (Gal. 4.6-7).

The Holy Spirit has called you to be free, to walk in his strength, to be informed and blessed by his Word. We are called to live free from condemnation, guilt, and blame. We no longer need to give in to our own selfish, sin-focused ways. We can form new habits of thought, experience new approaches to living, and have new ways of relating to others. Because the Holy Spirit lives within us, we are not obligated to follow the passions of our old sinful nature. You have a choice; you can live by those things the Holy Spirit wants you to do or, by the inclinations of your old sin nature. Whatever we choose, there will be a harvest (Gal. 6.7-9).

Choose life! Walk in the Spirit and not by the flesh. Ask the Holy Spirit to strengthen you. Stay in his Word (the Scriptures), and talk to him constantly. Obey him promptly in all the things he asks you to do. Don't be discouraged, either. The more you "keep in step with" the Holy Spirit, the easier it will be to listen to him, obey him, and follow his leading.

Affirmation

The Holy Spirit indwells me, giving me guidance and strength to do his work with freedom and confidence so that the Church may grow in unity and maturity to the glory of God.

Prayer

John Chrysostom (349 – 407) was an important leader of the early Church, known for his captivating preaching and public speaking. In fact, his nickname (Chrysostom) comes from the Greek word "Chrysostomos," which means "golden-mouthed."

Prayer for Mercy, Slavonic Liturgy of John Chrysostom

In peace, let us pray to the Lord.
    Lord, have mercy upon us.
For peace from on high, and for the salvation of our souls,
let us pray to the Lord.
    Lord, have mercy upon us.
For the peace of the whole world, for the good estate of the holy churches of God, and for the union of all, let us pray to the Lord.
    Lord, have mercy upon us.
For this holy house, and for those who with faith, reverence and godly fear enter therein, let us pray to the Lord.
    Lord, have mercy upon us.
For our [bishops and other] clergy, and for the congregations committed to their charge, let us pray to the Lord.
    Lord, have mercy upon us.
For our country, for all its people, and for those who are entrusted with civil authority, let us pray to the Lord.
    Lord, have mercy upon us.
For this city, and for all the cities and countries, and for those who in faith dwell therein, let us pray to the Lord.
    Lord, have mercy upon us. Amen.

~ Roger Geffen. *The Handbook of Public Prayer*. p. 115.

Heart Cry to the Lord

O, Spirit of God, the Spirit of the Father and of his Son, Jesus Christ, you are God, the Third Person of the Blessed Trinity. You are the Spirit of truth, of love, and of holiness, and we know that you were sent to us from the Father at the request of our Lord Jesus. Because I have trusted in Jesus, you have come to me, and now I adore you, and love you with all my heart. Thank you for living in me, for sealing me as God's own possession, and teaching me the Word of God that I might know and seek God as my light and strength. You are my strength.

Fill my heart with love for the Lord, and the fear of God. Lead me into the ways of the Lord, and overcome in me any false desire to sin or forsake your will and work. Grant me patience and clarity, in order that I might not fall into sin, and increase my faith, that I might cling to you, depend on you, and through you, become more like Jesus my Lord. So change my life that it can become a holy life, the life that you've called me to live, and help me please you, heavenly Father, in all things. You are my Source, who together with Jesus and the Spirit reign as one God. Through Jesus Christ, my Lord, I pray. Amen.

For More Study

At www.tumi.org/sacredroots, we have a section dedicated to additional written and video resources.

Go to www.tumiproductions.bandcamp.com and download the song, "Spirit of God," an anthem seeking the power of the Holy Spirit in our lives.

Foster, Richard J. and James Bryan Smith Eds. *Devotional Classics: Revised Edition: Selected Readings for Individuals and Groups.* Renovare, Inc. (HarperCollins Publishers), New York. 1993.

For the Next Session

In the next session, you will explore **The Excellence We Show** including these topics:
1. We are to imitate God as dearly loved children.
2. As ambassadors, we are to represent God as a holy, thankful people.
3. We are to live a life of love and service to others.

Scripture Memory

Philippians 2.13

Assignments

1. Ask to meet with a pastor, elder, or deacon to find out ways you can serve in your church.
2. Ask two mature believers in your church what they think their spiritual gifts are, and how they came to discover them.
3. Select a way to serve and start serving in the local church.

THE EXCELLENCE WE SHOW
Living as Saints of God and Ambassadors of Christ in This World

> Therefore be imitators of God, as beloved children. And walk in love, as Christ loved us and gave himself up for us, a fragrant offering and sacrifice to God. But sexual immorality and all impurity or *covetousness** must not even be named among you, as is proper among *saints**. Let there be no filthiness nor foolish talk nor crude joking, which are out of place, but instead let there be thanksgiving. For you may be sure of this, that everyone who is sexually immoral or impure, or who is covetous (that is, an *idolater**), has no inheritance in the kingdom of Christ and God.
>
> ~ Ephesians 5.1-5

Objectives

By the end of this session, you should embrace the *Excellence We Show* by believing that:

- We are to imitate God, as his own dearly loved children.
- As saints (holy ones) in Christ, we are to represent God before others as his own holy, thankful people.
- As ambassadors, we are to share the Good News of salvation with our friends, families, and neighbors, demonstrating in good works the love of Christ in service to others.

. . . .

*covetousness – Covetousness is an intense desire to possess something or someone that belongs to someone else. It is more than just wanting something, but is an extreme greed that comes from self-centeredness and an arrogant disregard for God's purposes.

*saints – A saint is someone who is set apart for God's possession, demonstrated in both service and worship. It is often misunderstood to mean someone whose behavior is extraordinarily good and religious. But the word "saint" and "sanctify" or "sanctification" are all based on the same idea: something that is set apart for a special purpose. For example, if you have a special dress or pair of shoes that you only wear for special occasions, that piece of clothing is "set apart" (or sanctified) for the purpose of special events. In the same way, "saints" are normal people who are set apart by God to worship and serve him.

*idolater – An idolater is someone who worships a created thing rather than worshiping the Creator. Because people want their lives to be good, and free of problems, they have tried to gain control of their circumstances by gaining the favor of powers they cannot understand. Therefore people worship form images of gods of the rain, weather, or victory in war, worshiping them instead of trusting in the Creator. Others are greedy for their own gain and put their trust in systems like capitalism, education, religious activity, or militarism. Therefore an idolater is anyone who seeks to get their needs met from anything other than God.

Opening Prayer for Wisdom

Eternal God, my Father, you say in your Word that you are the source of all knowledge and wisdom. I acknowledge this as the truth, dear Father, and I ask that you impart into me divine wisdom, that I may be able to rightly divide the Word of truth (2 Timothy 2.15). Please instruct and teach me in the way I should go (Psalm 32.8), and direct my steps. Incline my ear to hear your voice, and correct me now in the way I think and speak, and lead me when I have gone astray.

Father, grant me the gift of discernment, and enable me as I study to know the difference between godly and ungodly teachings, spirits, and gifts. Show me by the Holy Spirit what your will is, and give me insight into how I can carry out your intentions with my whole heart.

Dear Lord, please help me to be quick to hear and listen, slow to speak, and slow to anger (James 1.19). Let the words of my mouth and the thoughts of my heart be acceptable in your sight. Allow me to speak your truth with wisdom in order that all with whom I speak may understand and benefit by your truth.

Teach me now in this study as I receive your Word and instruction. I ask for these things in the strong name of Jesus, my Lord and Savior, Amen.

Contact

1. **"Where do I get the strength to do that, I mean, to be like him?"** As a part of his past life, a young Christian was a part of a gang that hated people of a particular race, the "Whites." Everything his gang did, everything they said, and everything they wanted related to blaming White people for what they had done to others down through history. The gang was dedicated to paying them back for the hurt and violence they had done to others, to put them down and hurt them whenever and however they could. On repenting and believing in Christ, this young Christian rejected this group and its hatred against Whites, but he was concerned about how he could keep himself from slipping back into the old habits of speech and conduct he lived for so long.

   After struggling with thoughts on this for some time, he said, "I don't want to be like I was, and I've come to better understand that the Lord wants me to be like him. But, honestly, *where* do I get the strength to do that, I mean, to be like him?" What would your advice be to this young, struggling Christian on this issue?

2. **"I've never been saintly, and, I don't think I'll ever be one of those kind of people. Me, a saint?"** In a Bible study with a young Christian (who actually was a middle-aged man), we happened upon the teaching that God expected us to live as saints (holy ones) in Christ. The

Scriptures were clear that we are to conduct ourselves in such a way that others can see that we represent God in what we do. We are called to live out our status as those who have been set apart for God's purpose and use, as his own holy, thankful people. The young Christian couldn't see how he could be like that, considering all the things that he had done, and the way he had previously lived. He was shocked that God would call him a "saint." How is it possible that we are called "holy ones" when we have done the kinds of things we have done in the past?

3. **"Being a Christian is like being a secret agent for the Kingdom of God!"** Perhaps you have seen the spy movies where a secret agent representing a foreign nation penetrates a situation and serves the interests of his country. Or, you have followed the news and heard an ambassador speak about the views of his country on a particular issue, relating to others the perspectives and policies of his country. When s/he was speaking, they were representing the position of their nation, literally speaking as if the entire nation was present and giving its official view on that issue. How does the Bible's use of the concept of ambassador help us to understand the role and duty of a Christian before their family, friends, associates, and neighbors, serving as the Lord's agent and ambassador of the Kingdom?

Content

In the last session (*The Endowment We Receive*) you learned that when you were saved, God the Holy Spirit gave you a gift(s) to be used to build up the Body of Christ. Now you will explore more fully how God intends to use you in creative ways to represent him in the world as you fight the good fight of faith.

Now that we have become the very children of God by faith in Jesus Christ (1 John 3.1-3), we are called to be like the Lord, to imitate God's character, to act like him, and to love others as if he were living through us right here on earth. We are called "saints," the very holy ones of God, made righteous through our faith in Christ, made holy and cleansed from sin by the blood of Jesus. God wills our *sanctification* (set apart for God's possession and use), that in every aspect of our lives – our thoughts and attitudes, speech, conduct, and our relationships – we might show others that we belong to Christ, and that his Kingdom can be seen among us, in the church.

We as believers in our various life contexts must *assume* the role of sainthood, and let the Holy Spirit, through time and discipline, form us into the very ones that the Father says we are. Each of us needs to learn how to control our own bodies in holiness and honor, for God did not invite us to a life of selfishness and lust, but to a new life that is both holy and beautiful – a life that glorifies him.

Furthermore, we have been made ambassadors for Christ, and God now makes his appeal to others through us. As we proclaim Jesus as Lord, and offer life in his name to all who believe, we can legitimize our message by the way we live, through our conduct, our speech, and our actions. Now, as his ambassadors, we are called to represent his interests, to speak his words, to behave differently than those who do not know him.

Rather than imitating the rest of the world, we show ourselves to be a transformed people, a thankful people. We are Christ's ambassadors. We turn our backs on a godless, sinful lifestyle and live a God-filled, God-honoring life, sharing with others the life given to us in Jesus Christ, our God and our Savior. We are his workmanship, set apart by God in order to bring glory to him through a variety of good works that he has prepared for us to do. We are to love and serve others, tell his story, and invite others to join us, especially those in our network of family and friends.

> It is clear here that there can be no separation of the advancing of the Kingdom of God from compassion, mercy, and justice. From this biblical foundation we must move the church to initiatives of compassion, mercy and justice. Compassion represents the love of God in us and flowing through us, and it creates our passion for lost people and the desire to see them experience new life. Mercy is our attitude toward broken people and broken communities. This is what gets us past the mind set of blaming and judging people for where they are. Even when people are in bad situations because of their bad choices, mercy leads us to respond in a way that is beyond what they deserve. It is the way God looked on us through someone else when we were living lives away from God.
>
> ~ Efrem Smith. *The Post Black & Post White Church: Becoming The Beloved Community in a Multi-ethnic World*. San Francisco, CA: Jossey-Bass, 2012, page 59.

The Excellence We Show
Lesson 5 Bible Study
Read the following Scriptures and answer briefly the questions associated with each biblical teaching.

1. *We are united to Jesus Christ as our life, and we bear fruit in our lives (living holy lives and sharing Christ's love) because we are in communion with (relating constantly to) him.* Read John 15.1-8 and answer the following:

a. In Jesus' understanding of the vine, the gardener, and the branches, who is Christ, who is the Father, and what are we?

b. If a branch fails to remain in him, ceasing to draw life and blessing from him, can that branch bear fruit?

c. How does Jesus say the Father is glorified in what we do?

2. *Everyone in Christ is a new creation, called to be holy and live as an ambassador for Christ where they live. Read 2 Corinthians 5.17-6.2.*

a. What ministry has God given us (v. 18)?

b. What did God do in Christ that makes transformation and new life available to all who believe? (v. 19)

c. What role do we play as we represent and make appeals in God's name to others (v. 20)

d. Describe the appeal we ought to make on God's behalf (v. 21).

3. *Those who believe are called to represent Christ and his kingdom glory before others in the world, in everything they do and say. Read Matthew 5.13-16.* Fill in the blanks:

a. We are the _____ of the earth

b. We are the _____ of the world.

c. Let your _____ shine so people can see your _____ and give glory to _____.

4. *Those who believe are to live as blameless and pure children of God, shining like stars in the midst of a dark and sinful world.* Read Philippians 2.12-16. Match the action with the corresponding truth.

a. Work out your own salvation   ___For it is God who works out his will in you

b. Do all things   ___As lights in the world

c. That you may be blameless and innocent   ___In the day of Christ [Paul] didn't run in vain

d. Among whom you shine   ___Without grumbling or questioning

e. Holding fast the word of life   ___Children of God without blemish

5. *God's will for each believer is that they might live a pure life, a life of holiness, following the guidelines laid out for us from the Master himself, Jesus Christ.* Read 1 Thessalonians 4.1-8. What does Paul say we should do to please God?

6. *As believers in Christ, we should set our minds on things above, and follow his rules for holy living as we live before others here below.* Read Colossians 3.1-17 and answer the following:

a. How are we to view ourselves, now that we have been joined to Christ? (vv. 1-4)

b. What attitude should we take about those things that belong to our "earthly nature?" (vv. 5-9)

c. What attitudes should we take regarding our old self and our new self? (vv. 9-10)

d. What kind of virtues should we cultivate, now that we are God's chosen people? (vv. 11-17)

7. God's grace instructs us how to live and to do good works as we prepare for the second coming of Christ. Read Titus 2.11-14. Fill in the blanks.

   a. The grace of God bringing salvation trains us to renounce _____ and to live _____ lives as we wait for our blessed hope.

   b. Jesus gave himself for us to redeem us from _____ and purify a people of his possession who are zealous for _____.

Summary

As God's beloved children by faith in Jesus Christ, we are called to be imitators of God, to be like our Lord, and to care for others in love. We are, as it were, his members here in this world, as if he were living through us, right here on earth. As such we are called to be "saints" (holy ones) of God, made righteous through faith in Jesus. We have been set apart to live lives that are pure and holy before the Lord. We are to be sanctified (set apart for God's possession and use), in order to both show and tell others that we belong to Christ, and that they too can be transformed through the same Gospel that has transformed us. Truly, God has not invited us to lives of ungodliness and impurity, but of holiness and righteousness.

In addition to being called to be saints, we have also been made ambassadors for Christ, representing Jesus and the Kingdom of God in our relationships and our conduct. We are agents of the Kingdom, citizens of the heavenly reign of God, and as such, have been empowered to make God's appeal to others in his name. We must be careful to do so with clarity, excellence, and boldness. In both word and deed we proclaim Jesus of Nazareth as both Lord and Christ, the coming King of the world. Through our Gospel presentations we offer life in his name to everyone who will repent and believe, and through our demonstration of love and good works we show what that Kingdom is about. Through our deeds, we play a godly version of "Show and Tell" every day before our family, friends, and neighbors, revealing to them what it means to be in the Kingdom of God.

No one can be a saint and an ambassador for Christ in their own strength and will. Christ lives in us by his Holy Spirit, and we can represent him only as we walk with him. As we depend on Christ, so can we represent him well.

Appendices

The Appendices you should study and meditate upon relevant to this lesson are the following:

The Oikos Factor (App. 10)
Communicating Messiah: The Relationship of the Gospel (App. 19)
Going Forward by Looking Back: Toward an Evangelical Retrieval of the Great Tradition (App. 16)

I am ashamed to think that any Christian should ever put on a long face and shed tears over doing a thing for Christ which a worldly person would be only too glad to do for money.

~ Hannah Witall Smith.
Richard J. Foster and James Bryan Smith, Eds.
Devotional Classics: Revised Edition:
Selected Readings for Individuals and Groups.
Renovare, Inc. (HarperCollins Publishers), New York. 1993, p. 239.

God calls us to work with him in transforming today's urban center into outposts of the city of God. Just as the Kingdom themes of *shalom* and land are very material, this-worldly realities, so God's concern is not with "mansions in the sky" but with liveable communities on earth. Finally he will bring his city and kingdom when the time comes to "restore everything" (Acts 3:21), and evil will be judged. But God's concern, and the present mission of the church, includes making the city a place of justice and peace *now*, rather than condemning and fleeing. This requires effective witness to the living Jesus Christ as both Savior and Sovereign Lord.

~ Howard A. Snyder. *Kingdom, Church and World: Biblical Themes for Today.*
Eugene, OR: Wipf and Stock Publishers, 2001, p. 48.

Key Principle

We are his workmanship, created in Christ for good works (Ephesians 2.10).

Case Studies | Read and reflect upon the following cases and concepts, and provide answers and insights into their resolution, based on the texts you studied above.

1. **What happens when we fail?** Often new believers find themselves enthusiastically accepting God's call to be his saints and ambassadors for Christ. As they walk with the Lord, they grow stronger, but, because of the world's temptations, the devil's lies, and their habits of living like the world in their old habits, they may fall short, and sin.

   What happens to us when we fail, or fail more than once, even in the same area? Is a person who claims to be a Christian and yet falls – does that person remain a believer? Are we kind of on a holy probation, where our salvation is in effect until we fail – then everything is cancelled out? Are they still considered a saint and an ambassador, even after they have done wrong? Read the following Scriptures, and share your answer with another believer, for input and direction:
   * 1 John 1.5-10
   * Prov. 24.16
   * James 5.16
   * Ps. 32.3-5
   * Prov. 28.12-13

2. **Is there a single Christian position on every issue in society?** Living as a saint of God and an ambassador for Christ is refreshing, but it is not simplistic or easy. We have to be careful not to confuse what we think with God's position on a particular issue, and we should be equally suspicious of simply accepting what the latest TV preacher thinks on a subject as the Gospel truth. There are equally sincere and godly Christians on opposite sides of any particular issue, with both sides quoting Scriptures, and claiming that their viewpoint represents the true "Christian" position. What is a Christian to do when they encounter strong believers who hold conflicting views on some particular question? Must there always be a single, clear, and "correct" opinion about every topic that comes up in society? How does Romans 14.1-12 help us understand these kinds of matters as we walk with the Lord?

3. **Who we are speaks louder than what we say.** Without question, who we are speaks louder than what we say before others. We must be careful not only to make verbal claims about the Kingdom of God, but actually live out those claims so that others may see and bear witness to the truth. The apostle John gives an example of this in his first epistle:

1 John 3.16-18 – By this we know love, that he laid down his life for us, and we ought to lay down our lives for the brothers. 17 But if anyone has the world's goods and sees his brother in need, yet closes his heart against him, how does God's love abide in him? 18 Little children, let us not love in word or talk but in deed and in truth.

The Bible is abundant in its call for believers to make their love genuine (Rom. 12.9), shown through our service to others (Gal. 5.13), not merely in nice words but in practical action (James 2.15-17). Why do you think the Lord places so much emphasis on the point that our love needs to be shown, not merely in words alone, but in practical good works that people can see and experience?

Connection

Now, you must think about what ways these dynamic biblical truths can impact your life right now. Since you are one of God's beloved children by faith in Jesus Christ, you have been called to become an imitator of God, and are called a saint, a holy one of God! Think of the ways that you currently conduct yourself, how you speak and react to others, how you relate to family members and friends, and how you care for others. Ask the Holy Spirit for strength and wisdom so you can live a life more consistent with God's call, with the people you relate to. What things do you need to quit doing, things that may block your experience with Christ, and leave a wrong impression on others regarding your testimony?

Also, you are an ambassador for Christ, called to represent Christ and his Kingdom in all you say and do. What ways can you better relate or act toward others that would give them a clearer picture of who Christ is, and what his Kingdom is about? Don't be afraid to be honest. You may have to stop some things altogether, maybe start doing certain things, or change certain behaviors or relationships. God may lead you to continue to do something, or ask you to do it more often, or with others. Be open to the Spirit as he speaks to you about your sainthood and your ambassadorship, and then do whatever he commands. Remember, godliness is simply obedience repeated in countless little ways, day after day after day. Respond to God as he speaks to you, and live into your new identity as a saint of God, and an ambassador of Christ.

Affirmation

Because of God's power at work within me, I can imitate God's character, representing God as his ambassador through love and service to others.

Prayer

Augustine of Hippo (354 –430), was a theologian and philosopher whose writings influenced the development of the Church in Western civilization. He was the bishop of Hippo (modern-day Algeria). He is viewed as one of the most important Church Fathers. Among his most important works are "City of God" and "Confessions."

Prayer to Know God, Augustine

Lord Jesus, let me know myself and know Thee,
    and desire nothing save only Thee.
Let me hate myself and love Thee.
Let me do everything for the sake of Thee.
Let me humble myself and exalt Thee.
Let me think nothing except Thee.
Let me die to myself and live in Thee.
Let me accept whatever happens as from Thee.
Let me banish self and follow Thee,
    and ever desire to follow Thee.
Let me fly from myself and take refuge in Thee,
    that I may deserve to be defended by Thee.
Let me fear for myself, let me fear Thee,
    and let me be among those who are chosen by Thee.
Let me distrust myself and put my trust in Thee.
Let me be willing to obey for the sake of Thee.
Let me cling to nothing save only to Thee,
    and let me be poor because of Thee.
Look upon me, that I may love Thee.
Call me that I may see Thee,
    and forever enjoy Thee.

~ Don L. Davis. *A Sojourner's Quest.*
Wichita, KS: The Urban Ministry Institute, 2010, pp. 93-94.

Heart Cry to the Lord

Eternal God, God and Father of my Lord Jesus Christ, thank you for calling me to be both a saint and an ambassador for Christ. I want to represent you in all I do, turning my back on the godlessness of this world, and reaching forward to the calling you have given me to live in your Kingdom to come. Please, Father, grant me the strength to be a saint, to live in holiness and in purity before you each day. Walk with me, and help me. Let me face each day with hope and confidence, knowing that your Spirit is with me, and that he will help me as I face the difficulties and challenges of the day.

As your saint, and as your ambassador, let me not lose contact with you today, and help me to remember in all things, that I do not belong any longer to myself. You bought me with a price, the blood of Jesus, and now

I belong to you. So, keep my mind and heart, in spite of all I may encounter today. Help others to see you through me, in what I do, how I act and react, and how I relate to everyone today. Open wide my eyes to see how I might bring more glory to you in all I do and say. These things I pray, through Jesus Christ, my Lord, amen.

For More Study

At www.tumi.org/sacredroots, we have a section dedicated to additional written and video resources.

Don L. Davis. *Vision for Mission: Nurturing an Apostolic Heart.* Wichita, KS: The Urban Ministry Institute, 2012. (This resource is available at *www.tumistore.org.*)

For the Next Session

In the next session, you will explore **The Edification We Seek** including these topics:
1. We live life together in community.
2. We worship Christ together in the local church and in small groups.
3. We submit to one another out of reverence for Christ.

Scripture Memory

Ephesians 2.10

Assignments

1. Take 10 minutes to make a list of ideas where you could be a better caretaker of what God has given you. Think about your money and possessions. List in your journal how they could be better used for the church.
2. Take 10 minutes to evaluate your life in terms of contentment. Where are you content versus where are you greedy or envious? Ask God where he is gently leading you to be content with your possessions or relationships and write about this in your journal.
3. Take 10 minutes to evaluate how you spend your time. Ask God how you might simplify your schedule so you are available to the Holy Spirit's leading. Write about this in your journal.
4. Talk to a mature believer about lessons they have learned about the use of money, greed, and a simple lifestyle.

THE EDIFICATION WE SEEK
Building Up One Another in the Body of Christ

> And do not get drunk with wine, for that is *debauchery**, but be filled with the Spirit, addressing one another in *psalms and hymns** and spiritual songs, singing and making melody to the Lord with your heart, giving thanks always and for everything to God the Father in the name of our Lord Jesus Christ, submitting to one another out of reverence for Christ.
>
> ~ Ephesians 5.19-21

Objectives

By the end of this session, you should embrace the *Edification We Seek* by believing that:

- The Christian life is designed to live life together in community, growing together as a family of God, the body of Christ, and the temple of the Holy Spirit.
- We learn of the things of the Kingdom, worship God, and grow as disciples of Christ as we relate to other believers in the local church and in small groups.
- As we follow Christ as Lord, we are built up (edified) in our faith as we learn how to submit to each other out of reverence (respect) for Christ.

Opening Prayer for Wisdom

Eternal God, my Father, you say in your Word that you are the source of all knowledge and wisdom. I acknowledge this as the truth, dear Father, and I ask that you impart into me divine wisdom, that I may be able to rightly

. . . .

*debauchery – Debauchery is excessive indulgence in pleasure. It doesn't mean we have to avoid everything that gives us pleasure but that we stay clear of reckless behavior that dishonors God. God has given us everything to enjoy, but everything has its proper limitations. For example, when a river is flowing within its banks, it is a powerful force for good, but when it overflows its banks and floods a town, that river gains destructive power. In the same way, debauchery is the improper use of God-given pleasure, when it overflows its boundaries and becomes destructive to the individual and those affected.

*psalms and hymns – Psalms are a certain kind of lyrical poem that are in the Bible that were sung in community, given as an expression of worship to God. Hymns and spiritual songs are expressions of love and worship that are both from the Bible and written by Christians through the ages.

divide the Word of truth (2 Timothy 2.15). Please instruct and teach me in the way I should go (Psalm 32.8), and direct my steps. Incline my ear to hear your voice, and correct me now in the way I think and speak, and lead me when I have gone astray.

Father, grant me the gift of discernment, and enable me as I study to know the difference between godly and ungodly teachings, spirits, and gifts. Show me by the Holy Spirit what your will is, and give me insight into how I can carry out your intentions with my whole heart.

Dear Lord, please help me to be quick to hear and listen, slow to speak, and slow to anger (James 1.19). Let the words of my mouth and the thoughts of my heart be acceptable in your sight. Allow me to speak your truth with wisdom in order that all with whom I speak may understand and benefit by your truth.

Teach me now in this study as I receive your Word and instruction. I ask for these things in the strong name of Jesus, my Lord and Savior, Amen.

Contact

1. **"Because of bad experiences I've had before, I just can't go to a church."** Unfortunately, many people have attended churches and have had awful experiences with others in them. Whatever the problems might have been – unforgiveness, grumbling and jealously, misunderstanding and personal hurt – they have been "turned off" to the prospect of going to another fellowship, and starting afresh in a new situation. Based on what you know right now, how would you advise a new believer about his or her attending a congregation to grow in Christ, especially if you learned that they had faced a horrible experience in another church?

2. **"I can't believe that the Bible is one continuous Story about God's rescue of his creation and humankind! Man, what a loving God we serve!"** You may know that the Bible is divided into two Testaments (the Hebrew Scriptures, 39 books, Genesis to Malachi), and the Christian New Testament (Matthew through Revelation, 27 books). What you might not be aware of is that although the Bible is a library of books, it is actually only a single, unfolding Story, one great drama that tells the tale of God's love for his creation and for humankind. It is only because of God's great love and commitment to his universe that we could be saved. In this respect, Christianity differs from virtually every other religion. Actually, religions tend to focus on practices, beliefs, or dogmas that people must follow in order to attain to a state of perfection, get a blessing, be transformed, or get protection. Christianity, on the other hand, is God giving salvation to humankind even though they don't

deserve it, didn't ask for it, and couldn't earn it. Why do you think it is so hard for people to get this basic message of the Scriptures? What might be hindering them from understanding the "grace of God," his royal love and mercy for all people, regardless of who they are, what they've done, and where they are?

3. **"How can our pastor lead all these people? I'll never get to know him!"** One of the things God says over and over in his Word is that we grow as we follow the teaching and the example of godly pastors and leaders he provides for us. In some churches, however, the pastor is leading a large group of believers, perhaps hundreds or thousands. With so many believers in the church, and with the pastors having so much responsibility, many complain that it becomes difficult if not impossible for every believer and every married couple and family to get to know the pastor intimately. "If getting to know your pastor well is a sign of being pastored, then I probably will never have a pastor," says one new believer. "How can our pastor lead all these people. I'll never get to know him!" What would you say to encourage this young believer in his understanding of what it means to be under pastoral care – how can it be done in today's church?

Content

In the last session (*The Excellence We Show*) you learned that we are to represent Christ as dearly loved children, to live both as saints of God and as Christ's ambassadors to a fallen world. Now you will explore how God intends for us to grow in our faith in the local church, under the authority of pastoral leadership, and in loving submission to one another so we can fight the good fight of faith.

Jesus wants his people to be unified and committed to one another as we live in community together. We gather weekly for worship, and meet together in Bible studies or small groups to build one another up. We must get to know other believers, and have them get to know us as well. We must learn to welcome one another in our homes, relax and play together, and do all we can to encourage one another as we follow Christ. As believers, we are called to live the Christian life, building up each other through the use of our gifts, our love, our friendships, and our conduct.

Moreover, we must be careful to challenge one another to love and good deeds, and to reject those evil things that we were formerly associated with before we became one of God's people by faith in Christ.

While all of us are constantly tempted to do evil, no place exists in the spiritual life or the Christian community for things that are associated with worldliness, things mentioned by the apostles in their letters to Christians – such as sexual immorality, impurity, lust, evil desires and greed.

Truly, we must rid ourselves of those things that do not edify (i.e., those things that tear down our spiritual walk), such things as anger, rage, malice, slander, and filthy language. As we learned in our last lesson, we truly have become the very saints of God, and are called to be ambassadors for Christ everywhere we go. Now we live to build up others, not tear them down or distract them in their love for Jesus.

Rather, we are called to build each other up as we pray for, challenge, and encourage one another in the church, following our spiritual leaders as they guide us through their teaching and example. As God's chosen people, we strive to love each other, and seek to cultivate new ways of living and thinking, learning how to live with compassion, kindness, humility, gentleness and patience. Above all else, our love for others must characterize our relationships with each other. In so doing, we will come to please Christ in all things.

The Edification We Seek
Lesson 6 Bible Study
Read the following Scriptures and answer briefly the questions associated with each biblical teaching.

1. *The Story of God involves the work of the Father, the Son, and the Holy Spirit, as told through the Bible, the Holy Scriptures. As believers in Christ, we are the people of that Story – we think about it in our "theology," sing and preach about it in our worship, are being formed by it in our discipleship, and tell others about it in our witness.* Read the following Scriptures, look at Appendix "The Story of God: Our Sacred Roots", and answer the questions associated with each text below.

    Our Objective Foundation: the Sovereign Love of God

    a. John 3.15-18. What role did the Father play in the Story of creation's salvation and rescue?

    b. 2 Cor. 5.18-21. What role did Jesus play in our salvation Story?

    c. Eph. 1.13-14. What role does the Spirit play in helping us apply God's Story?

    d. 2 Timothy 3.15-17. How do the Scriptures help us understand God's Story?

Our Subjective Response: Salvation by grace through faith

e. Rom. 10.9-10. How do we as believers, the Church, first respond to the Story?

f. 1 Pet. 2.8-9. What is the goal of our worship – what is our primary purpose in Christ?

g. Col. 2.6-10. How are we formed by the Story – who or what do we focus upon?

h. Matt. 28.18-20. What command has Christ given the Church as she lives in the world?

2. *Having the full assurance of faith in the Lord Jesus Christ, and our sure hope of forgiveness in God's Story, we ought to find practical ways to encourage and build up other believers.* Read Hebrews 10.19-25. Fill in the blanks:

a. We should consider how to stir up one another _____ _____ (v. 24)

b. We should not neglect _____ as is the habit of some (v. 25)

c. We should _____ and all the more as we see the Day drawing near (v.25).

3. *Having been saved by the grace of Christ, we are in a new Story owning a new identity and expecting a new destiny. Therefore, believers should no longer imitate the lifestyle of those who do not know the Lord, but should conduct themselves as those who have been redeemed by Christ.* Read 1 Peter 4.1-11 and write out four exhortations Peter gives the believers to do as God's chosen people.

a.

b.

c.

d.

4. *The way we relate to other believers should reflect the same attitude of humility that Christ displayed in winning our salvation for us.* Read Philippians 2.1-11. What does Paul say our attitude should be like?

5. *The new commandment that Christ has given to his disciples is that we love one another, laying down our lives in sacrifice for each other.* Read 1 John 3.11-18. Match the phrase with the corresponding truth.

    a. This is the message you have heard   ___We should love one another

    b. Do not be surprised   ___That Jesus laid down his life for us

    c. We know we have passed from death into life   ___But in deed and truth

    d. By this we know what love is   ___Because we love our brothers

    e. Whoever does not abide in love   ___The world hates you

    f. Let us not love with word or talk   ___Abides in death

6. *Now that we belong to Christ and live into his very own Story, we ought to walk worthy of the salvation he has given us, knowing that we are united in one body and one Spirit.* Read Ephesians 4.1-6. List three qualities we are to display to live in a manner worthy of the calling we have received.

    a.

    b.

    c.

7. *As people of the Story of God, believers should be careful how they live, follow the Holy Spirit, and build one another up in worship and thanksgiving to God through Christ.* Read Ephesians 5.15-21 and match the command with the description.

a. Look carefully how you walk   ___To the Lord with your heart

b. Addressing one another   ___To God the Father in the name of Christ

c. Singing and making melody   ___Not as unwise but as wise

d. Giving thanks always   ___In psalms, hymns, and spiritual songs

e. Don't be foolish   ___But understand what the will of the Lord is

8. *God has granted godly leaders to watch over the souls of believers in the church, those charged to teach us and lead us into the richness of the Story and in fellowship with other believers.* Match the following Scriptures with the correct answer.

a. Hebrews 13.7   ___Obey your leaders and submit to them respectfully

b. Hebrews 13.17   ___Consider the outcome of your leaders lives, and imitate them

c. 1 Thess. 5.12-13   ___Respect and esteem your leaders, those who admonish you in God

9. *The enemy lies about our sufficiency in Christ, suggesting that God is holding something back from us. But God's Word affirms we have everything we need for life and godliness.*

a. Read Genesis 3.1-7. What lie did the serpent tell Eve that led her to believe God was holding back from her?

b. Read 2 Peter 1.3. Fill in the blanks: Through his _____ _____ he has given us _____ we need for _____.

> It is very important for us to associate with others who are walking in the right way – not only those who are where we are in the journey, but also those who have gone farther. Those who have drawn close to God have the ability to bring us closer to him, for in a sense they take us with them.
>
> ~ Teresa of Avila.
> Richard J. Foster and James Bryan Smith, Eds.
> *Devotional Classics: Revised Edition:*
> *Selected Readings for Individuals and Groups.*
> Renovare, Inc. (HarperCollins Publishers), New York. 1993, p. 165.

Summary

God wants every believer in Christ to be built up (edified), to grow to maturity in Christ, and to learn what it means to build up others. Jesus desires for us to grow up in our faith through our participation in the local church, an assembly of believers. We are commanded to learn under the example and teaching of godly pastors, and to live together with other Christians in loving submission to one another so we can fight the good fight of faith.

God's only method for this way of growth is his loving, Christian community – a local church. We now play our part in the Story of God! We are each provided spiritual gifts that we are to cultivate in service to the Body, building up one another as we gather each week as Christ's worshiping community, and as we meet together in Bible studies or small groups. God intends for us to love one another as Christ has loved us. This is something we learn to do together, as we are led by the Holy Spirit and the shepherds (pastors) God gives to lead and feed us. We must strive to be friends with other believers, welcome them into our lives and our homes, and spend time relaxing and playing together. We are family, and must learn to relate as members together.

Furthermore, we are also called to challenge one another to love and to practice good deeds, and to reject those evil things that we were formerly associated with before we became one of God's people by faith in Christ. We only fight the good fight when we fight it with other Christian soldiers, in healthy Christian community, under the direction of godly leaders who admonish and encourage us through their example and the Word of God.

Appendices

The Appendices you should study and meditate upon relevant to this lesson are the following:

Our Declaration of Dependence: Freedom in Christ (App. 9)
Fit to Represent: Multiplying Disciples of the Kingdom of God (App. 20)
The Oikos Factor (App. 10)

Key Principle

My command is this: Love each other as I have loved you (John 13.34).

Case Studies

Read and reflect upon the following cases and concepts, and provide answers and insights into their resolution, based on the texts you studied above.

1. **"What spiritual gifts do I have, and how can I use them?"** The Bible says that every Christian is given spiritual gifts which allow him or her to edify (build up) others in the Christian community (Rom. 12.3-8; 1 Cor. 12.4-11; Eph. 4.9-15; 1 Pet. 4.10-11). These gifts are to be utilized in a body of believers, as they interact, live together, engage in service, and grow together under a pastor's care. Why is it always more important to serve with and care for others than to argue and quibble about what our particular gift might be?

2. **"Why should I join a church as a member when I feel fine just attending services each week?"** In discussing the role of the local church in discipleship and building up (edifying) other Christians, one new believer began to discuss her own experience with church involvement. "I love attending the church I am going to now. I love the worship and the pastor's preaching, and their services are short and sweet. Frankly, I have not actually thought about joining the church, as a member, I mean. I know others who only attend the Sunday service, and don't go to small groups, or other events. I like this. Why should I join a church when I feel fine just attending there each week?" Based on what you have learned in this study, what would you say to this sister in the Lord about the necessity of being a deeper part of a church than only its Sunday morning worship service?

3. **"Making friends isn't easy with Christian people."** One of the difficulties many people have faced in attending church is the lack of personal friendships. It is truly surprising how many people are active

in their local churches but do not have a single intimate friend within its members. To begin with, friendship is important but costly. If you are to have friends you must be open to relating to people in love (Prov. 17.17), be willing to be known and understood (John 15.13-14), and be open to receive input, even criticism, on things you may need correction on (Prov. 27.6). Friends provide the kind of warmth and counsel we need in order to grow in Christ (Prov. 27.9). The use of spiritual gifts among each other can be like the sharpening of a file on a knife: "Iron sharpens iron, and one man sharpens another" Proverbs 27.17. Given these truths, what is most important for you right now to do if you are going to form strong, meaningful relationships with others in your local church?

Connection

Jesus wants us to grow as disciples and to fight the good fight of faith of spiritual warfare, not by yourself but with other believers, in community together. If you have not attended church regularly, make a commitment right now to become a member of a fellowship. Ask mature believers where they gather with others each week for worship, and then make a commitment to go. Inquire about their new members class, and begin attending a Sunday School class and/or a small group, Bible study, or cell group. Don't be discouraged, but determine that you will be patient as you get to know other believers, use your gifts to build them up, and learn from them as well.

Also, make an effort to get to know your pastors (or leaders, or elders, however they may be named in your church). Let them know that you attend the church, and will be praying for them. Ask for a visit, and share with them who you are. Help your leaders lead you better: "Obey your leaders and submit to them, for they are keeping watch over your souls, as those who will have to give an account. Let them do this with joy and not with groaning, for that would be of no advantage to you (Heb. 13.17)." Make up your mind to be a strong believer in the community with others. God will give you grace as you press forward with them into a strong Christian life together.

Affirmation

Because Jesus has commanded his disciples to love one another, I commit myself to life in church community, forgiving and submitting to one another.

Biblical Christianity is by God's plan universal in nature; it can take on itself the identity of any culture. We see this universality of the Gospel in the book of Acts. The day of Pentecost, when the gospel was preached in every language of the world, is clear proof that the Christian gospel is not locked into a particular culture or language. We see its universality as it was communicated and absorbed in Jewish and Greek cultures in the first century. The call of the church was to penetrate every nation, every culture, with the message of salvation, that all peoples might submit to God in their ethnicity. So, in Christianity, if I do not worship God *in my own culture*, I am being inconsistent with my faith.

~ Carl F. Ellis, Jr.
Beyond Liberation: The Gospel in the Black American Experience.
Downers Grove, IL: InterVarsity Press, 1983, p. 137.

Prayer

Francis of Assisi (1181 – 1226) was an Italian church leader and preacher. He organized a group of people dedicated to preaching and living a life of poverty for the sake of Christ and serving others, called the Franciscan Order. He helped organize other orders throughout his lifetime. He is one of the most respected Christians in history.

Prayer of Dedication, Francis of Assisi

Lord, make me an instrument of your peace.
Where there is hatred, let me sow love,
Where there is injury, pardon
Where there is doubt, faith,
Where there is despair, hope,
Where there is darkness, light,
Where there is sadness, joy.

O Divine Master,
grant that I may not so much seek to be consoled as to console,
not so much to be understood as to understand,
not so much to be loved, as to love;
for it is in giving that we receive,
it is in pardoning that we are pardoned,
it is in dying that we awake to eternal life.

~ Don L. Davis. *A Sojourner's Quest.*
Wichita, KS: The Urban Ministry Institute, 2010, pp. 95.

Heart Cry to the Lord

Eternal God, God and Father of my Lord Jesus Christ, thank you for placing me within the body of Christ. Thank you that I do not have to live my Christian life on my own, without the support of others who also love you, and who are seeking to please you. Thank you for the way you build up your people in the local church, and for giving to us leaders and pastors whose teaching and example help us know and do your will. Grant me grace to be patient with others, to learn from them, and to listen to their criticism and counsel. Help me to overcome any tendencies to separate myself from them, to hide or be apart from them. I need them if I am going to be what you want me to be, so give me courage to persevere with others, and always to gather with them, never shunning nor neglecting them. Teach me through my leaders, and encourage and challenge me through fellow believers. In doing so, I know that I will grow up to maturity in your Son. Thank you, Father, for the gift of your people. In Jesus' name I pray, amen.

For More Study

At **www.tumi.org/sacredroots**, we have a section dedicated to additional written and video resources.

Don L. Davis. *Sacred Roots: A Primer on Retrieving the Great Tradition.* Wichita, KS: The Urban Ministry Institute, 2010.

For the Next Session

In the next session, you will explore **The Enemy We Fight** including these topics:
1. We do not wrestle against flesh and blood.
2. Our enemy the devil works through the fallen world and the desires of the flesh.
3. Our enemy leads his minions to employ common schemes to discourage and distract us.

Scripture Memory

John 13.35

Assignments

1. Find two mature Christians and ask them to share about their experience in getting guidance from God through the counsel of others in the church. Ask them what mistakes they have made by not getting advice from other believers.
2. If you have not already done so, determine within the next month to start attending a single church regularly, a place where you can begin to fellowship and decide if God wants you to become a member. Remember, you cannot be edified (or edify others) if you are not in a local church, under the authority of godly pastoral leadership.

3. Develop a list of areas where you need guidance. Pray daily for a week that God would guide you in these areas, speaking through his Word and through other believers.

4. Seek out two mature believers to share your list with and ask them for their counsel.

THE ENEMY WE FIGHT
Walking in Victory Against the Enemy of God

> For we do not wrestle against flesh and blood, but against the rulers, against the authorities, against the cosmic powers over this present darkness, against the spiritual forces of evil in the heavenly places.
>
> ~ Ephesians 6.12

Objectives

By the end of this session, you should embrace the reality of the *Enemy We Fight* by believing that:

- The universe is at spiritual war, the devil and the kingdom of darkness versus the Lord Jesus Christ and the Kingdom of light: we "do not wrestle against flesh and blood."
- Christ has won the victory over our enemy, the devil, who still continues to work through deception in this fallen world system and our old sinful nature, i.e., "the desires of the flesh."
- We can overcome our enemy if we acknowledge Jesus' victory over sin on the Cross, be watchful of the devil's attempt to deceive us, and cling to the promise of God in order to stand our ground against our enemy.

Opening Prayer for Wisdom

Eternal God, my Father, you say in your Word that you are the source of all knowledge and wisdom. I acknowledge this as the truth, dear Father, and I ask that you impart into me divine wisdom, that I may be able to rightly divide the Word of truth (2 Timothy 2.15). Please instruct and teach me in the way I should go (Psalm 32.8), and direct my steps. Incline my ear to hear your voice, and correct me now in the way I think and speak, and lead me when I have gone astray.

Father, grant me the gift of discernment, and enable me as I study to know the difference between godly and ungodly teachings, spirits, and gifts. Show me by the Holy Spirit what your will is, and give me insight into how I can carry out your intentions with my whole heart.

Dear Lord, please help me to be quick to hear and listen, slow to speak, and slow to anger (James 1.19). Let the words of my mouth and the thoughts of my heart be acceptable in your sight. Allow me to speak your truth with wisdom in order that all with whom I speak may understand and benefit by your truth.

Teach me now in this study as I receive your Word and instruction. I ask for these things in the strong name of Jesus, my Lord and Savior, Amen.

Contact

1. **"Those folk don't belong to God – aren't those people the enemies of the Lord?"** In a world where religious war and violence are everywhere, it is easy to think, at first glance, that our battle is against human beings. Around the world, people claiming to know God are killing others who they deem to be heretics, or evil. To be sure, human beings are doing horrible things to one another throughout the world, from reckless violence to cruel indifference. But, according to the Bible, our fight is not against flesh and blood (human beings) but against spiritual forces who work through people to do terrible things within God's creation. Why might this truth be important for a new or growing Christian to understand and apply?

2. **"The devil's non-secretive secret weapon."** The Bible is clear that the devil's warfare is not like the kind that Hollywood is fond of portraying in horror films – grotesque, monstrous figures chasing innocent, vulnerable folk in dark alleys and haunted houses. At the core of the devil's most effective weapons are *lies*; polished arguments that seem harmless, believable, and even trustworthy. These lies suggest that God does not exist, that spirituality is made up, and that science alone can save humankind from its plights. It turns out that the secret weapon of our enemy is not secretive at all. Put simply, the devil is a liar and the father of lies. Why do you think the devil has chosen lies and deception as his primary weapon in *our* society, one which is so oriented to scientific proof and technological discovery?

3. **"Though you have the victory, you need to fight for it."** One of the things that the apostles emphasized in their teaching is that we need to play our part in God's Story. Simply put, even though God is conquering our enemy, the devil, he must and can be resisted. Even though Jesus won the victory for us on the Cross, the victory is not automatic. Although God has freed us through the shed blood of Jesus Christ, we now need to apply that victory by affirming truth and rejecting lies. As we do, we will be changed and transformed in our conduct, relationships, and

attitudes. This victory is ours, but it must be fought for, defended, and applied each moment of every day. God instructs believers to submit to him, to resist the devil, and only then will the enemy flee from us. Why do you think the Lord would have us receive our victory only after we have engaged the enemy and resisted his attempts to hurt, deceive, and defeat us?

Content

In the last session (*The Edification We Seek*) you learned that we are to love one another and submit to one another in the local church. Now you will find out more about the enemy we face in the good fight of faith.

Because of Satan the universe is at war, and we are combatants in this war. Neutrality is not possible. Our adversary the devil leads a host of spiritual beings who are clever and dangerous. They use the fallen nature of the world and the desires of our own flesh to resist God's work, so we must be on our guard against their schemes. We must also realize that no human is our enemy. Even though we experience spiritual danger at every turn, God is with us and helps us fight the good fight of faith, despite the efforts of the enemy.

Though Jesus has won the victory over the devil for all Christians, we still must take on an attitude to fight the enemy, to be self-controlled and alert. We must be vigilant and watchful, for our adversary (the devil) is constantly looking for an opportunity to harm us, to attack us, and to destroy us. Through lies and accusations he seeks to maul, discourage, and devour believers, to spiritually defeat us as we follow Christ.

We must, therefore, learn how to effectively resist the devil, to withstand him. We must defend ourselves against his attacks, telling ourselves the truth, making sure that we depend completely on Christ. We must walk in the power of the Holy Spirit, and stand firm in the truths of our faith. Remember, too, that we are never alone in this fight; other Christians scattered through-out the world are also suffering in their own warfare, too.

We can be certain that although the battle is fierce, constant, and daily, in the end, the grace of God will provide the ultimate victory. Our suffering will last only a little while, but the glory we will experience in Christ will be eternal. God himself will restore us, make us strong, help us to stand firm, and keep us steadfast, till the end of the fight!

> Though you and I have stepped from the kingdom of darkness into the kingdom of God's dear Son, we are still surrounded by a culture controlled by God's great enemy, Satan. We must live in it from the moment we accept Christ as our Savior until judgment falls. We, too, are encompassed by one who was once our king but is now our enemy. It is just plain stupid for a Christian not to expect spiritual warfare while he lives in enemy territory.
>
> ~ Francis Schaeffer.
> *The Complete Works of Francis Schaeffer*
> *Volume 2: Joshua and the Flow of Biblical History.*
> Westchester, IL: Crossway Books, 1975, page 210.

The Enemy We Fight
Lesson 7 Bible Study
Read the following Scriptures and answer briefly the questions associated with each biblical teaching.

1. *The devil has opposed God's will and Kingdom from the beginning, and God has determined that this rebellion would be put down by a Savior to come.* Match the following Scriptures with their correct phrasing:

   a. Gen. 3.1-15   ___ The entire world is under the devil's control

   b. Isa. 14.12-17   ___ The devil was created perfect, but he rebelled against God

   c. Ezek. 28.12-17   ___ The devil determined to make himself just like the Lord

   d. 1 John 3.8-10   ___ Jesus came to earth to destroy the works of the devil

   e. Rev. 12.7-11   ___ He is called Satan, the deceiver of the whole world

   f. 1 John 5.19   ___ The devil lied to the first human pair, causing the Fall

   g. 2 Cor. 2.11   ___ The devil uses common tactics so we can be aware of his schemes

2. *Jesus came to overcome, defeat, and destroy the works of the devil – to liberate humankind from the curse brought upon it by its disobedience to God.* Read Luke 11.14-23 and answer the following questions:

   a. When Jesus cast out demons, what did people accuse Jesus of doing?

   b. How did Jesus reply to the charge that he cast out demons through the power of the prince of demons, Beelzebul?

   c. Jesus gave an illustration about the need for the "strong man" to be overcome in order for his goods to be taken. Explain the meaning of this statement.

3. *The devil uses lies, accusation, and deception as weapons to trick, harm, and discourage believers as they represent Christ in the world.* Match the following Scriptures to their proper description.

   a. John 10.1-18   ___Jesus is the good shepherd, but the enemy comes to steal, kill, and destroy the sheep

   b. John 8.31-44   ___The devil is a liar and the father of lies

   c. Rev. 12.9-10   ___The devil accuses Christians before the throne of God

   d. Col. 2.15   ___Jesus defeated the devil on the cross, and put him on display

4. *Believers are to be sober-minded, watchful, and aware because even though the devil has been defeated, he is seeking those whom he can devour.* Read 1 Peter 5.8-11 and fill in the blanks.

   a. We are to be _____ and _____ for the devil's workings (v. 8).

   b. The devil prowls around like a _____, seeking someone _____ (v.8).

   c. We are called to _____ in the faith, knowing that the same kind of _____ are being experienced by our brothers and sisters throughout the world (v. 9).

d.   When we've endured the fight, God will himself 1) _____,
2) _____ , 3) _____ , and
4) _____ us in our faith (v. 10).

5.   *We must not love the world or the things in the world; to do so is to reject the love of the Father for us.* Read 1 John 2.15-17 and answer the following questions.

a.   True or False. If anyone loves this world, the love of the Father rests and rules in that person.

b.   What three things come from the world and are not from the Father?

   i.   The desires of _____

   ii.   The _____ of the eyes

   iii.   The _____ in possessions

c.   What does John say about the state of the world? What does he say about the person who does the will of God?

6.   *The Holy Spirit in us will give us the power to live for God, and to avoid the pitfalls of our old nature and temptations of the world. He enables us to live victorious in Christ.* Read Romans 8.1-17. Fill in the blanks:

a.   There is no condemnation for those who are _____ (v. 1).

b.   You are not in the _____ but in the _____ (v. 9).

c.   We are debtors, not to the flesh, to _____ _____ (v. 12).

d.   You did not receive a spirit of _____ but the Spirit of adoption as _____ (v. 15).

7.   *Not every assertion we hear about Jesus or his work is true. We must, therefore, test the spirits, for greater is the One who indwells us.* Read 1 John 4.1-6.

a. How can you test the spirits, i.e. how can you recognize the Spirit of God? (v. 1-3)

b. The Holy Spirit (the One who is in you) is greater than the one who is in the _____ (v.4).

8. *We must not be surprised or overwhelmed when we are misunderstood, rejected, or even hated by others because of our faith. We follow in the footsteps of Jesus, who experienced the same things.* Read the following Scriptures and answer the questions.

a. Read John 15.18-21. Why does the world hate us?

b. Read 1 John 3.11-15. Why should we not be surprised if the world hates us?

c. Read James 4.1-7. What must we do to ensure that the devil (the one who controls the world) will flee from us?

Summary

According to Scripture, the devil and the first human pair rebelled against the rule and government of God, and their rebellion thrust the universe into war. Since the fall of humankind in the Garden of Eden, God has determined to defeat the devil and all rebellion in his creation by sending his Son into that very same creation. Jesus entered our world – to put down the devil, pay the debt for our sin, and restore the fulness of the Kingdom of God. Thanks be to God, because of the work of Jesus of Nazareth, in this world, the devil has been defeated, and the Kingdom of God has come, and is being offered to all who believe!

Now that we have believed in Christ, we have been delivered from the kingdom of darkness and translated into the Kingdom of his dear Son (Col. 1.13). We have now joined the fight; we are combatants in this war. We are called to represent our Lord, the Victor over the powers of evil that have harmed God's creation. In this war, no one can remain neutral. Our adversary, the devil leads and directs spiritual beings who seek to destroy peoples' lives with cleverness and deception. This fallen world system works together with our own internal desires to undermine God's will in our lives. We are called to be sober-minded and watchful, aware of the devil's efforts to oppose us and harm us. We can resist him through the power of the Spirit, as we cling to the truth of God's word, rejecting his lies as they come to us. God will strengthen us as we fight the good fight of faith!

The centrality of Christ to all of history and to the meaning of human existence invites us into Jesus Christ, through whom we read the entire Bible from beginning to end. As pastors of the Word, there is a strong need to soak ourselves in the Triune story of God with its detailed exposition of the central role of Christ in the greatest drama of human history – *the drama of God who becomes one of us to rescue the world*. This theme of God's rescue of us all – not inspirational topics, motivational speakers, or massive therapy sermons – needs to be recovered as the central message of our church. This is not only the apostles' way of reading and preaching the Scriptures, it is also the way of the ancient fathers and, for the most part, the churches that do an ancient-future worship.

~ Robert E. Webber.
Ancient-Future Worship: Proclaiming and Enacting God's Narrative.
Grand Rapids, MI: Baker Books, 2008, p. 121.

Appendices

The Appendices you should study and meditate upon relevant to this lesson are the following:

The Theology of Christus Victor (App. 11)
Christus Victor: An Integrated Vision for Christian Life and Witness (App. 12)
Jesus of Nazareth: The Presence of the Future (App. 4)
Jesus Christ, the Subject and Theme of the Bible (App. 22)
Let God Arise! The Seven "A's" of Seeking the Lord and Entreating His Favor (App. 23)

Key Principle

Do not be surprised at the painful trial you are suffering as though something strange has happened (1 Peter 4.12).

Case Studies

Read and reflect upon the following cases and concepts, and provide answers and insights into their resolution, based on the texts you studied above.

1. **"I'm trying to understand what 'standing firm in the faith' means, but I'm not sure I get it."** After a great study of the Bible with friends, a young Christian was meditating on the meaning of 1 Peter 5.8-9: "Be sober-minded; be watchful. Your adversary the devil prowls around like a roaring lion, seeking someone to devour. *Resist him, firm in your faith*, knowing that the same kinds of suffering are being experienced by your

brotherhood throughout the world." She was trying to understand what it meant to be firm in your faith. In the study she had heard the leader say that the word "resist" here in this text was the Greek term *antistete*, the same one used in Ephesians 6.11-13 and James 4.7. It means to remain faithful, trusting in God's Word, even if things seem to be going opposite of what you think. She was struggling, with tough questions. "Does that mean that I can't or shouldn't doubt? What if I become discouraged? What if I slip and fall – can I get back up?" How would you counsel this young sister to understand this concept?

2. **"Why would God allow the devil to keep harassing and hurting us, even after our Lord Jesus has already won for us the victory?"** One of the more puzzling ideas for new believers to understand is why it is necessary for believers to stand firm in their faith against the lies of the enemy, if Jesus has won the victory. Surely, Jesus has defeated the devil on the Cross (Col. 2.15), and believers have overcome him through the blood of the Lamb and the word of their testimony, loving not their own lives to the death (Rev. 12.9-10). Why, then, do they still need to fight? Why is God allowing the devil to fight against his people, even after Jesus destroyed his works in his first coming (1 John 3.8)? (Hint: Jesus said that the servant is not greater than his master, cf. John 13.16.)

3. **"Nobody can understand the kind of pain and heartache that I have gone through. Nobody."** When we face difficult times, heartache, or loss, we are often tempted to think that no one else has ever gone through testings or trials similar to our own. The nature of pain and loss is intimate and personal; our hurt and struggles can be so fierce that we are inclined to think that no one else has ever felt the way we do, that nobody could possibly understand the level of hurt, discouragement, and despair that we are facing. A number of texts in the Bible suggest that this is simply not the case. However difficult our trials, they are similar to the tests and trials that other believers around the world are facing. Look at 1 Cor. 10.13 (ESV): "No temptation has overtaken you that is not common to man. God is faithful, and he will not let you be tempted beyond your ability, but with the temptation he will also provide the way of escape, that you may be able to endure it." How can our understanding of this truth help us endure trial in the face of difficult times?

Connection

Thanks be to God who has given us the victory through our Lord Jesus Christ (1 Cor. 15.57)! We have been rescued from the power of the devil, delivered from the kingdom of darkness, redeemed through the blood of

Jesus on the Cross, welcomed as members of a new government, boasting a new authority and Kingdom of God's dear Son (Col. 1.13). This great victory is ours, but we must learn how to resist our enemy, to join the good fight, and struggle as combatants in this war. Think of the areas where you have been called to represent *Christus Victor* (a title given to Jesus which means "to Christ be the victory") – in your family, among your friends, in your neighborhood, on your job, and with those whom you encounter. You are now a soldier of Christ (2 Tim. 2.1-8), and called to stand your ground in the face of our enemy's constant attacks.

One of the first things we must learn in this warfare is how to align our self-talk with the teaching of the Word of God. It is not the *circumstances* that we encounter but the *thoughts we tell ourselves* that shape and influence both what we feel and how we act. We must now learn to tell ourselves the truth about this great battle, about our identity, about Christ's victory, and about the resources the Lord has given us to help us gain the victory. Since the thoughts we tell ourselves (those things we believe) determine how we behave, we must learn brand new habits of speaking to ourselves. We must learn to agree with God, affirming Jesus' victory over the power of evil, and believing that when we submit to God and resist the devil's lies, the devil will flee.

Start right now (today), to ask the Holy Spirit to make you aware of the lies you have been believing. Determine to interpret your life based on the truth of the Word of God and your victory in Christ, not by how things look or how you feel. Learning new habits of thought will take time, so be patient. The more you affirm the truth and claim the victory that is yours in Jesus, the stronger you will get, making you more effective in spiritual battle. Begin today, asking God to grant you strength as you form new attitudes, new habits, and new patterns of thinking. As you do, you will live into the victory Jesus has won for you, prevent discouragement and emotional upset, and grow up into maturity in your Christian life.

Affirmation

I have an enemy that attempts to discourage me from my kingdom work, so I will not be surprised when trials come.

Prayer

Anselm of Canterbury (1033 – 1109), was born in France and was later a Church leader in England. He is called the "founder of scholasticism" because of his influence in theology. He is famous as the originator of the "ontological argument" (explaining the existence of God).

Prayer for Instruction, Anselm

O Lord my God,
Teach my heart this day where and how to see you,
Where and how to find you.
You have made me and remade me,
And you have bestowed on me
All the good things I possess,
And still I do not know you.
I have not yet done that
For which I was made.
Teach me to seek you,
For I cannot seek you
Unless you teach me,
Or find you
Unless you show yourself to me.
Let me seek you in my desire,
Let me desire you in my seeking.
Let me find you by loving you,
Let me love you when I find you.

~ Don L. Davis. *A Sojourner's Quest.*
Wichita, KS: The Urban Ministry Institute, 2010, p. 98.

Heart Cry to the Lord

Dear Heavenly Father, God and Father of the Lord Jesus Christ, thank you for the victory you have given your children over the adversary, the devil. Your love for us allowed you to give the gift of your Son, and now we have been delivered from his kingdom of darkness and delivered into the Kingdom of your Son. You have forgiven me of my sin, made peace with me through the blood of the Cross, and given me eternal life in his name.

Thank you, dear Father, that I am now your child, that your Holy Spirit leads and guides me, and that I can walk in victory in Jesus' name. Lead me not into temptation, but deliver me from all evil. My only desire is that you be praised and glorified in who I am and what I do. Give me grace today that I may please you, for you alone are worthy of my praise. In the name of Jesus I pray these things, amen.

For More Study

At www.tumi.org/sacredroots, we have a section dedicated to additional written and video resources.

Neil T. Anderson. *Victory over the Darkness.* Bloomington, MN: Bethany House Publishers, 2013.

For the Next Session

In the next session, you will explore **The Equipment We Use** including these topics:

1. God gives us weapons so we can stand our ground.
2. We must believe truth and stand against lies.
3. We develop our capacity to fight through the practice of spiritual disciplines.

Scripture Memory

John 16.33

Assignments

1. Set a goal to review this material at least three times this next week. Practice telling yourself the truth in the form of speaking simple truths out loud as you go through the day. For instance, you could say, "Thank you, heavenly Father, for overcoming the devil and his ways in my life through my faith in Jesus Christ" or "This thought is not from the Lord. It is a lie, and I will not accept it." You will form new habits of self talk as you practice walking by faith during the day.
2. One of the ways we defeat the enemy is through the discipline of fasting. Fasting is giving up food or some other regular activity to give special focus to God and the good fight of faith. Give up one meal to pray, study and meditate on God. (If your own health limitations are such that you cannot skip a meal, give up a television show or a planned recreational activity instead.)
3. Record your experience of fasting in your journal and share it with a mature believer in the church.
4. Plan your next fast and put in on your schedule.

THE EQUIPMENT WE USE
Putting on the Whole Armor of God

> Therefore take up the whole armor of God, that you may be able to withstand in the evil day, and having done all, to stand firm. Stand therefore, having fastened on the belt of truth, and having put on the breastplate of righteousness, and, as shoes for your feet, having put on the readiness given by the gospel of peace. In all circumstances take up the shield of faith, with which you can extinguish all the flaming darts of the evil one; and take the helmet of salvation, and the sword of the Spirit, which is the word of God.
>
> ~ Ephesians 6.13-17

Objectives

By the end of this session, you should embrace the *Equipment We Use* by believing that:

- God has provided every believer with the armor they need in order to resist the enemy and stand their ground when under attack.
- The truth of Scripture (i.e., the Word of God) can enable us to identify, stand against, and replace the lies that the enemy hurls against us.
- The Holy Spirit develops our capacity to fight the enemy through our practice of the spiritual disciplines.

Opening Prayer for Wisdom

Eternal God, my Father, you say in your Word that you are the source of all knowledge and wisdom. I acknowledge this as the truth, dear Father, and I ask that you impart into me divine wisdom, that I may be able to rightly divide the Word of truth (2 Timothy 2.15). Please instruct and teach me in the way I should go (Psalm 32.8), and direct my steps. Incline my ear to hear your voice, and correct me now in the way I think and speak, and lead me when I have gone astray.

Father, grant me the gift of discernment, and enable me as I study to know the difference between godly and ungodly teachings, spirits, and gifts. Show me by the Holy Spirit what your will is, and give me insight into how I can carry out your intentions with my whole heart.

Dear Lord, please help me to be quick to hear and listen, slow to speak, and slow to anger (James 1.19). Let the words of my mouth and the thoughts of my heart be acceptable in your sight. Allow me to speak your truth with wisdom in order that all with whom I speak may understand and benefit by your truth.

Teach me now in this study as I receive your Word and instruction. I ask for these things in the strong name of Jesus, my Lord and Savior, Amen.

Contact

1. **"Everybody is involved in a spiritual war? That sounds like a little bit of Hollywood stuff to me!"** In discussing the pastor's sermon on spiritual warfare with an unbelieving friend, a young disciple of Christ had her first encounter with real doubt about the reality of spiritual things. Debbie's friend, Ralph, had been listening to Debbie share with him her faith in Christ, how Jesus died on the Cross in order to pay the penalty of humankind's sin, defeating the powers of the enemy, who through fear of death had kept humankind subject to bondage. "What did you say, Deb? Do you believe that we are in some kind of spiritual battle?" Debbie replied, "Yes, the Bible says that the entire universe is at war, and that the real enemy of people are not each other, but the Evil One, Satan, whose lies and deception have caused people to rebel against God and hurt each other." "I don't know if I can swallow that, Deb. You mean that everybody is involved in a spiritual war? That sounds like a little bit of Hollywood stuff to me!" How would you counsel Deb to respond to her friend Ralph about the reality of spiritual warfare?

2. **"Lies are the deadliest weapons of the world, stronger than the strongest missiles."** This is the sentiment of one of the best Bible teachers the world has ever known, Rev. Dr. John Stott. He taught much on the meaning of Scripture, and believed that in the spiritual warfare that every disciple of Jesus is engaged in, the heart of the fight is over the truth, i.e., what is actually the right interpretation of the world, life, and things to come. He argued that the truth of Scripture (i.e., the Word of God) can enable us to identify, stand against, and replace the lies that the enemy hurls against us. What do you think of this phrase: "Lies are the deadliest weapons of the world?" Can you think of some examples in history of lies that people believed that led to horrible things being done or perpetrated on others, simply because people accepted falsehoods as the truth?

3. **"The more you do it, the better you get at doing it."** All of us are creatures of habits, which, as it turns out, winds up being among one of the most useful traits that human beings have. The principle is fairly simple. The more you practice a certain attitude, thought, practice, or behavior, the easier it is to repeat it--, and normally, the better one

becomes at doing it. In the same way, God has granted us certain practices that form us spiritually (often times called disciplines) which increases our capacity to fight the enemy. The more we practice the disciplines of the Christian life (e.g., pray, fellowship with other believers, read, study and memorize the Scriptures, and worship God), the stronger we get and the easier it is both to recognize the enemy's lies and to resist them by faith. Read Gal. 6.7-9. How does this text help us understand how we can grow to maturity in Christ through our steady, patient practice of the spiritual disciplines?

Content

In the last session (*The Enemy We Fight*) you learned about the nature of the enemy. In this session you will learn how to utilize the "whole armor of God," the equipment that the Lord has given us to fight our good fight of faith.

The true nature of the Christian life is warfare, not against people but against the spiritual forces of evil who withstand our work because we belong to Christ. We ought never be surprised that the enemy is relentless; his attack will be both fierce and constant. God has provided us the proper armor, the full arsenal of spiritual weapons for us to use in spiritual warfare. The fight we are in is portrayed as a struggle with spiritual forces who are determined to see us compromise our faith, surrender our commitment to Christ and replace it with worldliness and distraction.

The Bible images the lies of the enemy as flaming missiles, arrows of the evil one, which can be extinguished by the shield of faith. Our faith in God is pictured as a shield that will protect us from the "the evil one," from Satan himself. Jesus is our Lord, Divine Warrior who defeated Satan in a mighty victory through the Cross and his resurrection from the dead. We stand victorious in the great Victor himself, *Christus Victor*, the Lord Jesus Christ.

Therefore, believers are spiritual warriors, soldiers of Christ, champions who are aware of what is at stake in the fight with the lies of the enemy. We must adopt a mind to fight the enemy, to represent Christ with honor in all that we do, and to stand our ground in the spiritual fight as we cling in childlike trust to the God and Father of our Lord Jesus Christ. Through him, we can withstand anything the enemy plots against us.

Since the most common tactic of the devil is to lie to us, our greatest weapon is to affirm the truth and refuse to believe lies, staying on the alert to falsehoods that we are tempted to accept. Each piece of the armor of God relates in some fundamental way to the truth of God in Christ. This is why we must learn about the various weapons of the armor, in order that through steady practice we can effectively employ them with skill against the enemy. The more we engage, the better we fight, as soldiers of Jesus Christ.

> Satan came into the Garden and whispered to Adam and Eve – and in them, to all of us – "You cannot trust the heart of God . . . he's holding out on you...you've got to take matters under your control."
>
> ~ John Eldredge. *Epic: The Story God Is Telling.* Nashville: Thomas Nelson, Inc., 2004, p. 55.

The Equipment We Use
Lesson 8 Bible Study

Read the following Scriptures and answer briefly the questions associated with each biblical teaching.

1. *While we live in the world, we do not wage spiritual war according to worldly standards; our weapons are from God, who trains us for effective spiritual warfare.* Read 2 Corinthians 10.3-5 and fill in the blanks regarding the weapons of our warfare.

   a. The weapons that God has provided us are not of the _____.

   b. These divine weapons have divine power to destroy _____.

   c. Through these weapons, we can destroy _____ and every _____ raised against the knowledge of God.

   d. Our use of the weapons allows us to _____ _____.

2. *God has supplied believers with the proper armor to stand firm against the schemes and strategies of our enemy, the devil, who uses lies to intimidate and harm believers.* Match the following Scriptures with their correct description:

   a. Rom. 13.11-12   ___The whole armor of God enables us to stand against the enemy

   b. Eph. 6.11-12   ___Cast off the works of darkness, put on the armor of light

   c. 1 Thess. 5.8   ___The breastplate of faith and love, and the helmet of salvation

3. *Believers are at war not only with the devil but also with what the Bible calls the "world," and the "flesh" (their own sin natures). Satan attacks believers externally through the temptations of this world system, and internally by causing believers to yield to their sinful inclinations.* Connect the Scriptures below with their correct interpretation:

    a.   James 4.4   ____The enemy seeks to undermine our commitment to Christ

    b.   Jude 3-4   ____To be friends with the world is to be God's enemy

    c.   2 Cor. 11.3   ____The devil accuses believers, seeking to condemn them before God

    d.   Rev. 12.10   ____Deception is the enemies weapon of choice to harm believers in their walk

4. *Believers are to take up the whole armor of God in order to withstand in the evil day, and after resisting the enemy, stand firm in the faith.* Read Ephesians 6.13-18. Match the parts of the armor of God with the things associated with each piece.

    a.   Belt   ____Of salvation

    b.   Breastplate   ____Of the Spirit, the Word of God

    c.   Shoes   ____Of readiness of the gospel of peace

    d.   Shield   ____Of truth

    e.   Helmet   ____Of faith

    f.   Sword   ____Of righteousness

5. *In our spiritual fight, the Lord is our strength and shield, equipping us to do battle against the lies, falsehoods, and deceptions of the devil.*

    a.   Read Matt. 4.1-11. How did Jesus resist the attacks and temptations of the enemy?

b. Read Psalm 18.31-48. Name three ways in which the Lord prepares his spiritual soldier to resist the tactics of the enemy:

i.

ii.

iii.

c. Read Ps. 144.1-10. How does the Lord teach us to fight the "enemies," i.e., the lies and falsehoods we face each day?

6. *The spiritual soldier must take up God's armor, and must cleanse himself or herself from all that hinders them from following him.* Read 1 Timothy 6.11-16. What should you pursue in order to fight the good fight of faith?

7. *Sin undermines our effectiveness in warfare, and can cause us to give up. Yet, if we sin, God has provided us with an advocate who represents us before the Father.* Read 1 John 2.1-2. If we sin, who is our advocate, speaking in our defense?

8. No matter how difficult and discouraging the battle against sin may become, the love of God guarantees that we can be victorious in the end. Read Romans 8.28-39. Fill in the blanks:

a. All things work together for _____ for those called according to his _____ (v. 28).

b. If God is for us who can be _____ us? (v. 31).

c. Who can separate us from the _____ of Christ? (v. 35).

d. In all these things we are more than _____ through him who loved us (v. 37).

e. List all the things that are powerless to separate us from the love of God that is in Jesus our Lord (v. 38-39).

9. *The sword of the Spirit is the Word of God, our God-breathed (inspired) Scriptures which are effective to outfit and prepare us for all we need to endure and persevere in our calling in Christ.* Read 2 Timothy 3.16-17. List three things the Bible does to equip us for every good work.

10. *In order to be effective in spiritual warfare, we must add to our faith the qualities of godliness that will make us productive throughout our Christian lives.* Read 2 Peter 1.3-11 and answer the following:

    a. What has his divine power granted us? (v. 3)

    b. Since we have his precious and very great promises, what do we partake in? (v. 4)

    c. After supplementing our faith with goodness, what else should we seek? (v. 5-7)

    d. How can we keep from being ineffective and unproductive in our knowledge of the Lord? (v. 8)

    e. What is true of someone who lacks these qualities? (v. 9)

Summary

Every believer in Jesus Christ is at war with the world, the flesh, and the devil. This is not violence against people or physical combat, but rather against the cosmic forces of wickedness who seek to deceive, distort, and destroy believers by use of falsehoods and deception. The devil prowls around like a roaring lion, seeking someone to devour (1 Pet. 5.8-9), and we should be on the alert, staying aware of his schemes and devices. His attacks against our minds and hearts will be fierce and constant.

In order to withstand the enemy in the day of battle, God has provided believers with heavenly armor, the "whole armor of God," given for our use in our spiritual warfare. The enemy's weapon of choice are lies, which the Bible pictures as flaming arrows of the evil one, which can only be extinguished by the shield of faith (one of the pieces of God's armor). In addition, we are offered the belt of truth, the breastplate of righteousness, the sandals of the Gospel of peace, the helmet of salvation, and the sword of the Spirit, the Word of God.

Never be discouraged as you engage in this spiritual warfare: "Share in suffering as a good soldier of Christ Jesus. No soldier gets entangled in civilian pursuits, since his aim is to please the one who enlisted him"

(2 Timothy 2.3-4). The attacks of the enemy in the form of lies, accusations, condemnations, and negativity can be constant. Learning to fight involves learning to be persistent, to be disciplined and faithful. The more you use the armor of God in your fight against the lies of the enemy, the more you will stand in his victory. Be patient and wait on the Lord.

Appendices

The Appendices you should study and meditate upon relevant to this lesson are the following:

How to Start Reading the Bible (App. 3)
Understanding the Bible in Parts and Whole (App. 13)
Summary Outline of the Scriptures (App. 17)
Chronological Table of the New Testament (App.18)
Communicating Messiah: The Relationship of the Gospels (App. 19)
Let God Arise! The Seven "A's" of Seeking the Lord and Entreating His Favor (App. 23)

> The real problem of the Christian life comes the very moment you wake up each morning. All your wishes and hopes for the day rush at you like wild animals. And the first job each morning consists simply in shoving them all back; in listening to that other voice, taking that other point of view, letting that other larger, stronger, quieter life come flowing in. And so on, all day. We can only do it for moments at first. But from those moments the new sort of life will be spreading through our system; because now we are letting Him work at the right part of us. It is the difference between paint, which is merely laid on the surface, and a dye or stain which soaks through and through.
>
> ~ C. S. Lewis.
> Richard J. Foster and James Bryan Smith, Eds.
> *Devotional Classics: Revised Edition:*
> *Selected Readings for Individuals and Groups.*
> Renovare, Inc. (HarperCollins Publishers), New York. 1993. p. 9.

Key Principle

The weapons of our warfare are not of the world (2 Corinthians 10.4).

Case Studies   Read and reflect upon the following cases and concepts, and provide answers and insights into their resolution, based on the texts you studied above.

1. **"Not everything that comes into your mind is from the Lord. Learn to check the sources!"** New believers must learn to understand that their mind is the battlefield of spiritual warfare. The enemy has access to our thoughts, and can suggest lies, falsehoods, or distortions to believers. If these deceptions are believed, they can cause emotional upset, false perspectives, and lead to destructive behaviors and habits. Although we possess the divine weaponry to resist the false ideas and perspectives we encounter, we still must learn how to "talk back to the devil," i.e., to use the Scriptures to combat particular lies the enemy flings at us.

   Read again the account of Jesus with the devil in Matt. 4.1-11. How did the Lord resist the temptations of the devil? What was his weapon? How did he respond to the wild claims that Satan gave him while in the desert? What can this teach us about our own spiritual warfare today?

2. **"I'll never be able to get out of this rut. Never."** In today's microwaved world, everyone is accustomed to getting what they need fast, quickly and directly. No one likes the idea of a long period of hard work before experiencing what they want, or what they feel they need. These kinds of attitudes can greatly impact the Christian life. Though the victory, deliverance, and protection has been granted through faith in Jesus (1 Cor. 15.57; John 5.24; Rom. 8.35-39; Eph. 1.3), we still need to learn how to fight, and how to wait for the victory.

   Young Christians are prone to become easily discouraged, especially when they began well, and then experience set back. Troubles, trials, and testings can prove to be difficult and exhausting, and can depress us. Even the strongest Christians can be caught off guard, and give in to the temptations and lies of the enemy. What do you think a believer should do when they get so down that they believe they can't get out of their rut: commit-the-sin, ask for forgiveness, commit-the-sin, ask for forgiveness again, and so on? What do you say to a growing Christian who believes that an area or issue is so hard for them that they think they cannot overcome it?

3. **"The key to success in the fight is perseverance. Your first and last lesson is to never give up."** In speaking about the struggles between the flesh and the Spirit with the Galatian believers, Paul summarizes his teaching in this way:

*Galatians 6.7-10 – Do not be deceived: God is not mocked, for whatever one sows, that will he also reap. For the one who sows to his own flesh will from the flesh reap corruption, but the one who sows to the Spirit will from the Spirit reap eternal life. And let us not grow weary of doing good, for in due season **we will reap, if we do not give up**. So then, as we have opportunity, let us do good to everyone, and especially to those who are of the household of faith.*

Paul says that we ought not grow weary in doing good. In other words, we ought not quit before we obtain our goals, spiritually speaking. He promised the Galatian believers that they would reap the rewards of their sacrifice if they did not give up. Everything in their warfare depended on them practicing what they had come to know, putting into practice the lessons of faith that Paul had taught them. If they refused to quit, he promised them that they would reap the rewards of their effort.

In thinking about yourself, what things cause you the most trouble, that cause you, more than anything else, to want to give up, give in, and to quit fighting? What can you do to ensure that you "stay in the fight" and resist the temptation to give up and give in to sin, lies, and temptation?

Connection

Yes, by faith you have been delivered from the kingdom of darkness, and have been translated into the Kingdom of our Lord Jesus Christ. Because of this, you are a spiritual warrior, a soldier of Christ, an enemy of the "cosmic forces over this present darkness." Although these enemies want to trap and harm you through their lies, falsehoods, and deceptions, you can learn, by faith and by practice, to discern and defeat them. By constant practice you can learn how to distinguish between what is good and what is evil (Heb. 5.11-14). Have no fear. As we take up God's armor, learn the truths of the Scripture, and live consistent with God's testimony about ourselves, we will mature.

The devil will try to stir you up and provoke you, but he will run away the moment you begin to pray. And above all, try to engage in useful work. In doing so, the devil is prevented from having access to you.

~ Thomas á Kempis.
Richard J. Foster and James Bryan Smith, Eds.
Devotional Classics: Revised Edition:
Selected Readings for Individuals and Groups.
Renovare, Inc. (HarperCollins Publishers), New York. 1993. p. 152.

How will this happen? Since the enemy's most common tactic is to get us to believe and act upon lies we hear, our greatest weapon (and our greatest armor against his attack) is to affirm the truth. Every believer must take up God's armor, keeping on the alert to falsehoods that they encounter, and resisting those lies by reciting and embracing the truth of Christ. What areas in your life today need to be rethought and reconsidered in light of the truth, i.e., what the Scriptures teach about it? What things are inconsistent with the truth in Christ? Reflect on Paul's threefold strategy of living in the truth:

> But that is not the way you learned Christ! – assuming that you have heard about him and were taught in him, as the truth is in Jesus, to put off your old self, which belongs to your former manner of life and is corrupt through deceitful desires, and to be renewed in the spirit of your minds, and to put on the new self, created after the likeness of God in true righteousness and holiness.
>
> ~ Ephesians 4.20-24

This text provides insight into how we can fight the good fight of faith effectively. First, put off the old man (with it lies and deceits); second, be renewed in the spirit of your mind (tell yourself the truth about that area); and third, put on the new man (act consistent with the truth until you form new habits of how to think, talk, and act around that issue). Meditate long on Paul's instruction to the Ephesians, and apply it daily.

What areas have you struggled in "putting off the old man (with its lies and deceits)"? In those areas, what must you "put off"? How will you renew your mind? How must you "put on the new self"? Ask the Spirit for wisdom and grace, and he will give you insight in your fight for the truth in these areas.

Affirmation

God has given me weapons to fight and so I must grow in my ability as a soldier of Christ through the practice of spiritual disciplines in the church, telling myself the truth, and refusing to believe lies.

Prayer

Teresa de Cepeda y Ahumada (1515-1582) was a Spaniard who began serving Christ as a nun at age 20. She was very devout and had a unique ability to write about her spiritual life. Her most famous work on prayer is "Interior Castle" in which she wrote following a deep intimate encounter with God.

Prayer for Surrender, Teresa of Avila

Govern all by thy wisdom, O Lord, so that my soul may be serving
Thee as Thou dost will, and not as I may choose. Do not punish me,
I beseech Thee, by granting that which I wish or ask, if it offend thy love,
which would always live in me. Let me die to myself, that I may serve thee,
who in thyself art the true life. Amen.

~ Don L. Davis. *A Sojourner's Quest.*
Wichita, KS: The Urban Ministry Institute, 2010, p. 98.

Heart Cry to the Lord

Eternal God, Lord and Master, thanks so much for your amazing grace in supplying us with your armor that can protect and outfit us as we encounter our enemies in this world. You did not leave us without aid in this great fight for your kingdom reign. We have your Holy Spirit, the forgiveness of Christ's blood, the armor of light, and the truth of the Scriptures, your Word. We have been placed in your family, have the wonderful promise and hope of eternal life, and have been given the gifts of your Holy Spirit. Help us, now dear Father, to use these wonderful gifts, to embrace your promise of eternal life, and to flee all lies, folly, and falsehoods as we learn to walk in the truth. Give us the strength to represent you with honor as we take up the whole armor of God, and learn to never give up, but rather to stand firm, in the evil day. In the name of Jesus I pray, amen.

For More Study

At www.tumi.org/sacredroots, we have a section dedicated to additional written and video resources.

William J. Backus. *Telling Yourself the Truth.* Grand Rapids, MI: Bethany House Publishers, 2000.

For the Next Session

In the next session, you will explore **The Endurance We Display** including these topics:
1. We must stay alert and not get caught off guard.
2. The Holy Spirit helps us in battle through prayer.
3. We help other believers in their fight.

Scripture Memory

2 Corinthians 10.4

Assignments

1. The enemy lies to us so we need to re-affirm the truth. Make a list in your journal of all the lies the enemy has told you recently: lies about your salvation, lies about God, lies about you, lies about others. Write out why these lies are untrue. Seek to find Scriptures which contradict these lies, expressing God's true claims about those areas.

2. Another way to fight the good fight of faith is through the discipline of confession. Take 10 minutes to pray, asking God to show any sinful way in you that you need to confess to God. After asking, be quiet and listen. If he brings sins to mind, simply agree with God and don't make excuses. Then receive his mercy and forgiveness, given by the shed blood of Christ.

3. Find a mature Christian and ask about their experience in confession and receiving forgiveness. Confess your sins to him/her and ask for words and prayers of forgiveness and healing from the brother/sister in Christ.

THE ENDURANCE WE DISPLAY
The Perseverance of the Saints

> Praying at all times in the Spirit, with all prayer and supplication. To that end keep alert with all perseverance, making supplication for all the saints.
>
> ~ Ephesians 6.18

Objectives

By the end of this session, you should embrace the *Endurance We Display* by believing that:

- The central principle of growing up into Christ is learning to persevere, to stay alert, and not get caught off guard; we must press on and continue forward for the prize, no matter how hard it may become.
- The Holy Spirit gives us power to stand true to our calling and commitment by helping us in our battles to persevere through prayer.
- As we stay true to Christ, and faithfully represent our calling, we can be used to strengthen other believers in their fight.

Opening Prayer for Wisdom

Eternal God, my Father, you say in your Word that you are the source of all knowledge and wisdom. I acknowledge this as the truth, dear Father, and I ask that you impart into me divine wisdom, that I may be able to rightly divide the Word of truth (2 Timothy 2.15). Please instruct and teach me in the way I should go (Psalm 32.8), and direct my steps. Incline my ear to hear your voice, and correct me now in the way I think and speak, and lead me when I have gone astray.

Father, grant me the gift of discernment, and enable me as I study to know the difference between godly and ungodly teachings, spirits, and gifts. Show me by the Holy Spirit what your will is, and give me insight into how I can carry out your intentions with my whole heart.

Dear Lord, please help me to be quick to hear and listen, slow to speak, and slow to anger (James 1.19). Let the words of my mouth and the thoughts of my heart be acceptable in your sight. Allow me to speak your truth with wisdom in order that all with whom I speak may understand and benefit by your truth.

Teach me now in this study as I receive your Word and instruction. I ask for these things in the strong name of Jesus, my Lord and Savior, Amen.

Contact

1. **"Why are so many Christians, even pastors, turning their back on their faith?"** Today, many people who profess to know Jesus as Lord are abandoning their faith, forsaking the church, and renouncing their spiritual calling in Christ. This is true not only for the rank-and-file folks in the pews of the church, but also those who are in the pulpit. Record numbers of churches are being closed, and many ministers are turning their back on the Scriptures and Christ. Many are trying to explain this pattern, while others seek to stop this outward flow by making Christianity more "fun" and more "relevant." Why do you think, at a time like this, so many are leaving the organized churches, and even professing that they no longer believe in Christ?

2. **"It has been tough, and I feel so disappointed in myself. I have actually thought of turning back and going to my old life!"** Many young believers often find themselves in an up-and-down cycle that goes between high times of commitment and love for Christ to low times of temptation and compromise with what they believe. It can be very discouraging for a new believer or a growing Christian to repeatedly fall, and then, to get up after each fall and continue on. In response to this cycle, the Scripture says, "For the righteous falls seven times and rises again, but the wicked stumble in times of calamity" (Prov. 24.16, ESV). The Christian life is tremendously worthwhile, but it is not easy. Why is it important for a growing disciple of Christ to be patient with herself or himself as they continue in their walk with God?

3. **"We learn obedience in the way Jesus did – through the things we suffer."** One of the hardest lessons for a new believer to learn is that the Christian life was never designed to be completely free of struggle, difficulty, and problems. We can feel betrayed when we learn what the psalmist said: Psalm 34.19: "Many are the afflictions of the righteous, but the LORD delivers him out of them all." If we were honest, we would prefer to never struggle, and rather avoid all forms of affliction and trial! Some of us feel hurt, and even cheated when we, as God's beloved children, have to endure so many heartaches and calamities. And, when you are a new Christian, you may find it tough to confidently persevere in the midst of such difficulties.

Yet, Scripture assures us that this is how Christ learned his lessons: Hebrews 5.7-8: "In the days of his flesh, Jesus offered up prayers and supplications, with loud cries and tears, to him who was able to save him from death, and he was heard because of his reverence. Although he was a son, he learned obedience through what he suffered." How can Christ's example provide us with hope as we learn to patiently endure our own particular trials in our faith journeys?

Content

In the last session (*The Equipment We Use*) you learned about the weapons of our warfare. In this session you will be encouraged to develop perseverance and endurance in the good fight of faith.

To endure something, we must not run away from it. We must determine in our hearts to follow a course of action that is consistent with what we believe and know. We must not surrender or turn around. Even if it gets difficult, troubling, and discouraging, we make up our minds to continue on, to press forward, to trust in God's promise and wait for his leading and strength. Perseverance, then, is a kind of holy stubbornness, a refusal to allow trials or tests to so discourage us that we turn our backs on our faith. Perseverance says, "No matter what, I will not abandon my commitment to the Lord."

Through the encouragement of other believers, prayer in the Holy Spirit, and belief in the promises of God, we can press on to attain our goals in Christ. We can honor our commitment to the Gospel and Kingdom of our risen Lord Jesus Christ only if we persevere. We can win, if we do not give up.

The perseverance of the good fight of faith, therefore, can be illustrated through the example of soldiers, athletes, and farmers (2 Tim. 2.1-8). Soldiers must learn to endure hardship, often doing without for long periods of time, being fatigued or bored, or being in danger. Athletes train under all kinds of weather and conditions, challenging themselves even when they are tired and hurt. Farmers patiently wait for the harvest, even though they cannot control the elements and conditions of the weather and crops.

Like these examples, so we must endure. We must be ready to try things and fail, and still try again, knowing that ultimately the battle belongs to the Lord. We can sow seeds, be patient, and learn to wait on the Lord. If we do, God will bring the harvest in due time.

Prayer is primarily a wartime walkie-talkie for the mission of the church as it advances against the powers of darkness and unbelief. It is not surprising that prayer malfunctions when we try to make it a domestic intercom to call upstairs for more comforts in the den. God has given us prayer as a wartime walkie-talkie so that we can call headquarters for everything we need as the kingdom of Christ advances in the world.

~ John Piper. *Let the Nations Be Glad.*
Grand Rapids, MI: Baker Academic, 2010, p. 65.

The Endurance We Display
Lesson 9 Bible Study
Read the following Scriptures and answer briefly the questions associated with each biblical teaching.

1. *Obstacles and enemies seek to prevent believers from growing to maturity and bearing fruit for Christ.* Read Matthew 13.1-9, and 13.18-23. List the four situations of the seeds, and match the statement with the description.

   a. Seeds that fell along the path   ___ They sprang up, were scorched, and withered

   b. Seeds on rocky ground   ___ They were choked by the thorns among them

   c. Seeds that fell among thorns   ___ Birds came and devoured the seeds

   d. Seeds that fell on good soil   ___ Produced grain, some 30, some 60, and some 100 times as much

2. *Since we are surrounded by so many who have persevered in their faith, we should lay aside everything that might hinder us, and allow Jesus to help us run our full course.* Read Hebrews 12.1-11. Fill in the blanks:

   a. Run with _____ the race that is set out for us (v. 1).

   b. It is for discipline that we endure hardship; when you are being disciplined, God is treating you as _____ (v. 7).

c. All discipline seems painful but later yields _____ to those who are trained by it (v. 11).

3. *We can learn to persevere by remembering the faithfulness of believers who endured under pressure in the midst of trials.*

    a. Read 1 Cor. 10.1-13. How are the examples of believers in Scripture meant to teach us about persevering in the faith?

    b. Read Job 23.8-14. What can we learn about the proper attitudes during struggle from Job's experience and reaction toward his trials and problems?

4. *Prayer is God's antidote and provision for every Christian who finds himself or herself in pain or struggle during troubled times.* Match the following verses with the correct description.

    a. Luke 18.1-8   ___Ask, seek, and knock in prayer, and God will supply

    b. 1 Thess. 5.17; Rom.12.12   ___You need to endure; do God's will, you receive the promise

    c. Luke 11.5-13   ___Pray without ceasing

    d. Heb. 10.36-38   ___We ought always to pray, and never to give up

    e. Eph. 6.18   ___Pray in all occasions, to bind up the pieces of the armor

5. *Believers are never to give up, but to constantly strengthen one another in our faith in the midst of trial.* Read Jude 20-25 and fill in the blanks.

    a. Jude says we should _____ in our faith and pray in the _____ as we wait for the mercy of the Lord that leads to eternal life.

    b. _____, waiting for the mercy of our Lord Jesus Christ that leads to eternal life.

6. *When we sow to the Spirit and persevere, we can reap a good harvest, but only if we do not give up.* Read Galatians 6.7-10. Fill in the blanks:

    a. God is not mocked, whatever one _____ that will he _____.

    b. Do not become weary of doing good, in due season we will reap if we _____.

7. *If we desire to live a godly life in Christ, it is inevitable that we will endure persecution, but God will strengthen us if we remain in his Word.* Read 2 Timothy 3.10-17 and list three things that are true about those who rely on Christ in trouble.

    a.

    b.

    c.

8. *As disciples of Jesus, we must learn to endure hardship like the soldier, the athlete, and the farmer.* Read 2 Timothy 2.1-8. Match the statement with the description. How do these images help us understand better the nature of the Christian life?

    a. What you heard me say   ___Crowned according to the rules

    b. Share in suffering   ___Entrust to the faithful who will teach others

    c. Compete as an athlete   ___Has the first share of the crops

    d. The hardworking farmer   ___As a good soldier of Christ

    e. Remember Jesus Christ   ___A descendant of David

9. *We should not be discouraged when we endure trials, but count it pure joy, knowing that God will use them to strengthen us; he will grant us wisdom to go through whatever we face.* Read James 1.2-8 and answer the following:

a. What should we do when we meet trials of various kinds? (v. 2)

b. What happens when steadfastness has produced its full effect? (v. 4)

c. If we lack wisdom in facing our trials and tribulations, what does God advise us to do? (vv. 5-8)

Summary

As fighters in the good fight of faith, we are called to endurance, to persevere until the end. To persevere is to go through something, to endure it, neither to hide nor run away from it. As Christians serving Christ in a hostile world, we face the constant temptation of this world system, the inner distraction of our sin nature, and the lying deception of the enemy, the devil. We are under stress, we face difficulties, we are misunderstood. In the midst of these trials, we must count it all joy as we endure them, knowing that the Lord will use them to train us how to wait upon him, and depend on his promise.

To persevere is to be stubborn in our faith, but to be so with holiness and confidence. We often have no insight about the reasons for our trials, but we trust God anyway. We must refuse to allow anything that we encounter to so discourage or wound us as to make us turn our backs on the Lord. To endure is to rely on God's power and provision to remain faithful in our commitment to the Lord. As we go through trials, we can be confident that God will supply our needs – through other believers, through prayer in the Holy Spirit, and through the encouragement of the Scriptures. As you finish this course, know that this is just the beginning. It is always too soon to quit, always too soon to compromise. Stand your ground, and watch the Lord meet your needs.

Appendices

The Appendices you should study and meditate upon relevant to this lesson are the following:

The Hump (App. 15)
Fit to Represent: Multiplying Disciples of the Kingdom of God (App. 20)
Ethics of the New Testament: Living in the Upside Down Kingdom of God (Principle of Reversal) (App. 21)
Let God Arise! The Seven "A's" of Seeking the Lord and Entreating His Favor (App. 23)

What we have now rediscovered, with a good deal of understandable enthusiasm, is that the same principles, which apply to science and athletics and music, apply equally to our religious experience. Once it was modish to claim absolute freedom in such matters, looking with condescension on those who were bound by a rule, but such condescension is now out of date. We cannot help but see that those who have a rule to live by seem to have more power available. . . . We are beginning to see the wonderful truth that a Christian is one who is harnessed, wearing Christ's yoke and thereby renouncing empty freedom. We see new significance in the Christian teaching that, whereas the way which leads to destruction is broad, the way which leads to life is intrinsically narrow. The Christian we now know, is not one who does as he pleases, but one, instead, who seeks to please the Lord.

~ Elton Trueblood. *The Yoke of Christ*. Waco, TX: Word Books Publisher, 1958, pp. 130-131.

Key Principle

Be faithful even to the point of death and I will give you the crown of life (Revelation 2.10).

Case Studies

Read and reflect upon the following cases and concepts, and provide answers and insights into their resolution, based on the texts you studied above.

1. **"I feel like I'm on a roller-coaster – I go up, I come down, I go up, I come down."** A young person who accepted the Lord just a few months previous, communicated frustration with the troubles and problems he was facing. He had begun to experience tensions with the folks at home, misunderstandings on the job, and constant pressures from temptations, like never before. This cycle of events had begun to discourage this young soldier of Christ, and he started to wonder if he had in fact accepted Christ "in the right way." Because he was experiencing so many issues, he thought "I feel like I'm on a roller-coaster – I go up, I come down, I go up, I come down. I am not very stable right now. I wonder if I am doing something wrong. A lot of Christians I know are not going through all this stuff like I am right now." In light of the verses you have just studied, what advice would you give to this new Christian about his situation and what he should do about it?

2. **"I don't see how I could make it without the people of God! They've made all the difference."** One fine brother in the Lord came to Christ in prison, and immediately after his release he made a commitment to a local church. He spent as much time with the believers in that congregation as he possibly could. He attended the services and studies, and became fast friends with other brothers in the church. He volunteered to serve in various outreach efforts of the church, and he sought the pastor's advice on matters he faced in his personal life. For years, this assembly of believers became his home, literally his home away from home, and in reflecting on how God used the pastor and the believers in that church in his life, he said, "I don't see how I could make it without the people of God! They've made all the difference. Their support, love, and counsel are the reason why I am serving the Lord today." How does this example help us to understand the role of other believers in our perseverance in our faith?

3. **"When will things begin to change? I've been struggling with this trial for such a long while. Man, it seems like a lot of waiting."** Sometimes the Christian life is exciting, with new lessons and victories coming one after another, producing in us feelings of surprise, excitement, and joy. At other times, however, it can be slow and difficult, filled with problems and trials that last a long time, with no relief in sight. Believers can easily become quickly discouraged after great pain, like suffering a prolonged illness, losing a loved one, or struggling with some moral failure. One of the most important lessons for Christian maturity is to learn how to wait on God *in the midst of difficult struggle*. We need God's grace to bring us *through* the trial, that we may endure it.

   This is why the disciplines of the Christian life are so important. Regardless of how we feel or how things are going, we need to persevere in prayer, in fellowship with Christ followers in a local church, in the Word of God, and in walking with the Lord. Why is it important to never let the things we are experiencing have the final say on our endurance through trial? Why is it dangerous to permit our emotions and reactions to circumstances to dictate how we follow Christ, whether in the disciplines, or in our walk with other Christians in fellowship?

Connection

Indeed, the central principle of growing up into Christ is learning to persevere, to stay alert, and not get caught off guard. We must press on and continue forward for the prize, no matter how hard it may become. But we don't do this alone. We have resources to empower us to stand true to our calling as we persevere in the good fight of faith. The Spirit of God encourages us – he constantly indwells us, works through other gifted believers to encourage us, and strengthens us in times of need. Every growing Christian endures stress and struggle, trials from within or without, but you must learn to persevere. Evaluate your times of prayer, in the Word, and your involvement in your church. What things does the Holy Spirit want you to do in order to strengthen your ability to persevere in your circumstances? Select one or two things, commit them to the Lord, and begin today, in the power of the Lord, to endure your trials. Remember, you are neither alone nor abandoned; all disciples are learning to endure (2 Tim. 3.12), and the Lord will never leave or forsake you (Ps. 27.1-3). Through the Lord and his strength, you can endure your trials, and honor Christ in all things.

Many nervous and emotional disorders are the accumulated result of years of self-indulgent living. I am not thinking of the drunkards or the libertines, but of the respectable Christians who probably would be horrified at the thought of touching liquor or of indulging in gross immorality. But they are nevertheless undisciplined, and the fatal weakness is unmasked in the day of trial and adversity. A lifelong pattern of running away from difficulties, of avoiding incompatible people, of seeking the easy way, of quitting when the going gets rough finally shows up in neurotic semi-invalidism and incapacity. Numerous books may be read, many doctors and preachers consulted, innumerable prayers may be offered, and religious commitments made; the patient may be inundated with drugs, advice, costly treatment, and spiritual scourgings; yet none lay bare the real cause: lack of discipline. And the only real cure is to become a disciplined person.

~ Richard Shelly Taylor.
The Disciplined Life: Studies in the Fine Art of Christian Discipleship.
Kansas City, MO: Beacon Hill Press, 1962, pp. i-ii.

Affirmation

Despite the opposition I face, I have been given power in the Holy Spirit to be alert at all times, enduring to the end and helping other believers to do the same.

Prayer

John Wesley (1703-1791), was one of 19 children born to Samuel and Susanna Wesley (who was a remarkable hero of faith herself). As a young man at college, he and his friends banded together to encourage one another to live a holy life, and others started calling them "Methodists" for their methodical approach. As a tireless preacher and organizer, focusing on the common folk in the English countryside, historians credit him for saving the country from a bloody revolution. His impact extended to beyond his death, where many Methodist preachers crisscrossed the American frontier with the gospel message.

Wesley's Covenant Prayer

I am no longer my own, but thine.
Put me to what thou wilt, rank me with whom thou wilt.
Put me to doing, put me to suffering.
Let me be employed for thee or laid aside for thee,
exalted for thee or brought low for thee.
Let me be full, let me be empty.
Let me have all things, let me have nothing.
I freely and heartily yield all things to thy pleasure and disposal.
And now, O glorious and blessed God, Father, Son and Holy Spirit,
thou art mine, and I am thine.
So be it.
And the covenant which I have made on earth,
let it be ratified in heaven.
Amen.

~ as used in the Book of Offices of the British Methodist Church, 1936.

Heart Cry to the Lord

Eternal God, Father of my Lord Jesus Christ, I believe in you as my God and my Savior. You have granted me eternal life in his name, and desire that I now live the Christian life as he did, remaining faithful and true to you to your Gospel and commandments. Grant to me the grace and help that only your Holy Spirit can provide, that through your Word, through prayer, through fellowship with other disciples in worship and the Lord's Supper, and by clinging to you I may I come to live more fully in the life you have given me. Help me to never give up, to always pray and rely on your strength, and to pursue your will with my whole heart, in order that you might be glorified, and your Kingdom come where I live and work. I love you, Father. Help me to persevere. In Jesus' name, I pray, amen.

For More Study

At www.tumi.org/sacredroots, we have a section dedicated to additional written and video resources.

Don L. Davis. *A Compelling Testimony.* Wichita, KS: The Urban Ministry Institute, 2012. (This resource is available at *www.tumistore.org.*)

Scripture Memory

1 Timothy 6.12

Assignments

1. Make a list of all the struggles, trials, and problems you are facing right now, and entrust each one to God. Ask the Lord for wisdom on how to respond to each, and seek counsel from your pastor or mature teachers as to how you can practically and specifically glorify God in each situation.

2. One way to grow in your ability to fight the good fight of faith is practicing solitude. We must learn to listen to God in silence. Take five minutes to be silent and wait for the Lord. Do not read or talk, just listen.

3. Ask a Christian friend to join you in this exercise: for each of the next six days, try to gradually extend your time of solitude so that after a week, you can sustain an hour of solitude.

APPENDIX

APPENDIX 1

ONCE UPON A TIME
The Cosmic Drama through a Biblical Narration of the World

Rev. Dr. Don L. Davis

From everlasting to everlasting, our Lord is God

From everlasting, in that matchless mystery of existence before time began, our Triune God dwelt in perfect splendor in eternal community as Father, Son, and Holy Spirit, the I AM, displaying his perfect attributes in eternal relationship, needing nothing, in boundless holiness, joy, and beauty. According to his sovereign will, our God purposed out of love to create a universe where his splendor would be revealed, and a world where his glory would be displayed and where a people made in his own image would dwell, sharing in fellowship with him and enjoying union with himself in relationship, all for his glory.

Who, as the Sovereign God, created a world that would ultimately rebel against his rule

Inflamed by lust, greed, and pride, the first human pair rebelled against his will, deceived by the great prince, Satan, whose diabolical plot to supplant God as ruler of all resulted in countless angelic beings resisting God's divine will in the heavenlies. Through Adam and Eve's disobedience, they exposed themselves and their heirs to misery and death, and through their rebellion ushered creation into chaos, suffering, and evil. Through sin and rebellion, the union between God and creation was lost, and now all things are subject to the effects of this great fall–alienation, separation, and condemnation become the underlying reality for all things. No angel, human being, or creature can solve this dilemma, and without God's direct intervention, all the universe, the world, and all its creatures would be lost.

Yet, in mercy and loving-kindness, the Lord God promised to send a Savior to redeem his creation

In sovereign covenantal love, God determined to remedy the effects of the universe's rebellion by sending a Champion, his only Son, who would take on the form of the fallen pair, embrace and overthrow their separation from God, and suffer in the place of all humankind for its sin and disobedience. So, through his covenant faithfulness, God became directly involved in human history for the sake of their salvation. The Lord God stoops to engage his creation for the sake of restoring it, to put down evil once and for all, and to establish a people out of which his Champion would come to establish his reign in this world once more.

So, he raised up a people from which the Governor would come

And so, through Noah, he saves the world from its own evil, through Abraham, he selects the clan through which the seed would come. Through Isaac, he continues the promise to Abraham, and through Jacob (Israel) he establishes his nation, identifying the tribe out of which he will come (Judah). Through Moses, he delivers his own from oppression and gives them his covenantal law, and through Joshua, he brings his people into the land of promise. Through judges and leaders he superintends his people, and through David, he covenants to bring a King from his clan who will reign forever. Despite his promise, though, his people fall short of his covenant time after time. Their stubborn and persistent rejection of the Lord finally leads to the nation's judgment, invasion, overthrow, and captivity. Mercifully, he remembers his covenant and allows a remnant to return – for the promise and the story were not done.

Who, as Champion, came down from heaven, in the fullness of time, and won through the Cross

Some four hundred years of silence occurred. Yet, in the fullness of time, God fulfilled his covenant promise by entering into this realm of evil, suffering, and alienation through the incarnation. In the person of Jesus of Nazareth, God came down from heaven and lived among us, displaying the Father's glory, fulfilling the requirements of God's moral law, and demonstrating the power of the Kingdom of God in his words, works, and exorcisms. On the Cross he took on our rebellion, destroyed death, overcame the devil, and rose on the third day to restore creation from the Fall, to make an end of sin, disease, and war, and to grant never-ending life to all people who embrace his salvation.

And, soon and very soon, he will return to this world and make all things new

Ascended to the Father's right hand, the Lord Jesus Christ has sent the Holy Spirit into the world, forming a new people made up of both Jew and Gentile, the Church. Commissioned under his headship, they testify in word and deed the gospel of reconciliation to the whole creation, and when they have completed their task, he will return in glory and complete his work for creation and all creatures. Soon, he will put down sin, evil, death, and the effects of the Curse forever, and restore all creation under its true rule, refreshing all things in a new heavens and new earth, where all beings and all creation will enjoy the shalom of the triune God forever, to his glory and honor alone.

And the redeemed shall live happily ever after . . .

The End

APPENDIX 2

THE STORY GOD IS TELLING

Rev. Don Allsman

Chapter Title	Chapter Summary	Theme Verse
An Attempted Coup (Before Time) Genesis 1.1a	God exists in Perfect Fellowship before creation. The devil and his followers rebel and bring evil into existence.	In the beginning was the Word, and the Word was with God and the Word was God. He was in the beginning with God. All things were made through him, and without him was not any thing made that was made (John 1.1-3).
Insurrection (Creation and the Fall) Genesis 1.1b – 3.13	God creates man in his image, who joins Satan in rebellion	Therefore, just as sin came into the world through one man, and death through sin, and so death spread to all men because all sinned (Rom. 5.12).
Preparing for Invasion (The Patriarchs, Kings, and Prophets) Genesis 3.14 – Malachi	God contends to set apart a people for his own, out of which will come a King to deliver mankind, including Gentiles. Clues to his battle plans are hinted at along the way.	They are Israelites, and to them belong the adoption, the glory, the covenants, the giving of the law, the worship, and the promises. To them belong the patriarchs, and from their race, according to the flesh, is the Christ who is God over all, blessed forever. Amen (Rom. 9.4-5).
Victory and Rescue (Incarnation, Temptation, Miracles, Resurrection) Matthew – Acts 1.11	The Savior comes to deal a disarming blow to his enemy.	The reason the Son of God appeared was to destroy the works of the devil (1 John 3.8b).
The Army Advances (The Church) Acts 1.12 – Revelation 3	The Savior reveals his plan of a people assigned to take progressive ownership from the enemy as they enjoy a foretaste of the Kingdom to come.	So that through the church the manifold wisdom of God might now be made known to the rulers and authorities in the heavenly places. This was according to the eternal purpose that he has realized in Christ Jesus our Lord (Eph. 3.10-11).
The Final Conflict (The Second Coming) Revelation 4 – 22	The Savior returns to destroy his enemy, marry his bride, and resume his rightful place on the throne.	Then comes the end, when he delivers the Kingdom to God the Father after destroying every rule and authority and power. For he must reign until he has put all his enemies under his feet. The last enemy to be destroyed is death (1 Cor. 15.24-26).
The War between the Kingdoms	The common thread of the Bible narrative is warfare.	The kingdom of the world has become the kingdom of our Lord and of his Christ. And he shall reign forever and ever (Rev. 11.15b).

It is a world where terrible things happen and wonderful things too. It is a world where goodness is pitted against evil, love against hate, order against chaos, in a great struggle where often it is hard to be sure who belongs to which side because appearances can be deceptive. Yet for all its confusion and wildness, it is a world where the battle goes ultimately to the good, who live happily ever after, and where in the long run everybody, good and evil alike, becomes known by his true name.

~ Frederick Buechner. *Telling the Truth*.

APPENDIX 3

HOW TO START READING THE BIBLE
Rev. Don Allsman and Rev. Dr. Don L. Davis

1. Read individual passage, texts, and even books in light of the context of the whole Story of the Bible. How does it fit in God's redemptive plan to win all that was lost at the Fall?

2. Observe the situation. Put yourself in the setting, noticing the surroundings, the sights, the smells. Imagine what it must have been like.

3. Pay attention to commands, warnings, instructions, and inspiration that shape how you live and think so you can seek his Kingdom first.

Ways to Read Through the Bible

Bible Reading Plan #1: From Genesis to Revelation
1. Start by reading through the book of John. This will give you an overview of Jesus' life and help you get some background as you read the rest of the Bible.

2. Go back to Genesis 1 and read straight through the Bible.

3. Do not get stuck on details, but read through the whole Bible to enjoy its richness and variety. Write down questions you have about words you don't understand or things that are confusing so you can ask someone or look them up later.

Bible Reading Plan #2: Chronological Reading Guide
(www.tumistore.org)
You also can read through the Bible each year, reading the various books in the order that Christian scholars believe it was written.

Many believers read through the Scriptures together every year "chronologically"(through time), seeking to gain greater insight on the entire Story of God *as it occurred in historical order of events.*

You may acquire a guide of this outline from *www.tumistore.org*. This simple listing of the books of Scripture will allow you to read through the Story of the Bible in the order the events happened. This will give you an overall sense of the Bible as one unfolding drama, and not as independent books disconnected from one another. It also helps we who read through the Bible each year stay on point regarding the true subject matter and theme of the Scriptures: the salvation of God in the person of Jesus of Nazareth, the Christ.

This guide will provide rich insight into the events of Scripture, and help you better comprehend the meaning of the whole story of God's wondrous salvation and grace, which climaxes in the Christ event, his death, burial, resurrection, ascension, and return.

Jesus of Nazareth: The Presence of the Future

Rev. Dr. Don L. Davis

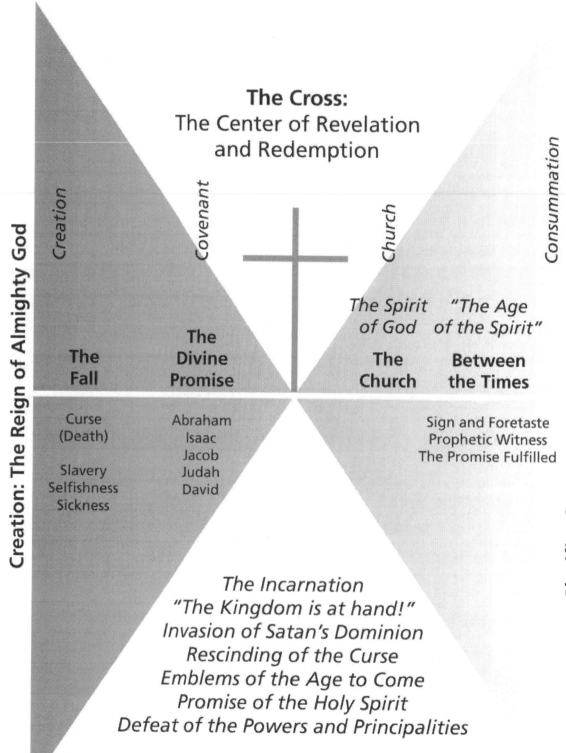

The Cross:
The Center of Revelation
and Redemption

Creation

Covenant

Church

Consummation

Creation: The Reign of Almighty God

Glorification: New Heavens and New Earth

The Fall

The Divine Promise

The Spirit of God   *"The Age of the Spirit"*

The Church   **Between the Times**

Curse (Death)

Slavery
Selfishness
Sickness

Abraham
Isaac
Jacob
Judah
David

Sign and Foretaste
Prophetic Witness
The Promise Fulfilled

The Incarnation
"The Kingdom is at hand!"
Invasion of Satan's Dominion
Rescinding of the Curse
Emblems of the Age to Come
Promise of the Holy Spirit
Defeat of the Powers and Principalities

APPENDIX 5

THE STORY OF GOD: OUR SACRED ROOTS

Rev. Dr. Don L. Davis

The Alpha and the Omega	Christus Victor	Come, Holy Spirit	Your Word Is Truth	The Great Confession	His Life in Us	Living in the Way	Reborn to Serve
The LORD God is the source, sustainer, and end of all things in the heavens and earth. All things were formed and exist by his will and for his eternal glory, the triune God, Father, Son, and Holy Spirit. Rom. 11.36.							
	THE TRIUNE GOD'S UNFOLDING DRAMA — God's Self-Revelation in Creation, Israel, and Christ			THE CHURCH'S PARTICIPATION IN GOD'S UNFOLDING DRAMA — Fidelity to the Apostolic Witness to Christ and His Kingdom			
	The Objective Foundation: The Sovereign Love of God — God's Narration of His Saving Work in Christ			The Subjective Practice: Salvation by Grace through Faith — The Redeemed's Joyous Response to God's Saving Work in Christ			
The Author of the Story	*The Champion of the Story*	*The Interpreter of the Story*	*The Testimony of the Story*	*The People of the Story*	*Re-enactment of the Story*	*Embodiment of the Story*	*Continuation of the Story*
The Father as *Director*	Jesus as *Lead Actor*	The Spirit as *Narrator*	Scripture as *Script*	As Saints, *Confessors*	As Worshipers, *Ministers*	As Followers, *Sojourners*	As Servants, *Ambassadors*
Christian *Worldview*	Communal *Identity*	Spiritual *Experience*	Biblical *Authority*	Orthodox *Theology*	Priestly *Worship*	Congregational *Discipleship*	Kingdom *Witness*
Theistic and Trinitarian Vision	Christ-centered Foundation	Spirit-Indwelt and -Filled Community	Canonical and Apostolic Witness	Ancient Creedal Affirmation of Faith	Weekly Gathering in Christian Assembly	Corporate, Ongoing Spiritual Formation	Active Agents of the Reign of God
Sovereign Willing	Messianic Representing	Divine Comforting	Inspired Testifying	Truthful Retelling	Joyful Excelling	Faithful Indwelling	Hopeful Compelling
Creator — True Maker of the Cosmos	Recapitulation — Typos and Fulfillment of the Covenant	Life-Giver — Regeneration and Adoption	Divine Inspiration — God-breathed Word	The Confession of Faith — Union with Christ	Song and Celebration — Historical Recitation	Pastoral Oversight — Shepherding the Flock	Explicit Unity — Love for the Saints
Owner — Sovereign Disposer of Creation	Revealer — Incarnation of the Word	Teacher — Illuminator of the Truth	Sacred History — Historical Record	Baptism into Christ — Communion of Saints	Homilies and Teachings — Prophetic Proclamation	Shared Spirituality — Common Journey through the Spiritual Disciplines	Radical Hospitality — Evidence of God's Kingdom Reign
Ruler — Blessed Controller of All Things	Redeemer — Reconciler of All Things	Helper — Endowment and the Power	Biblical Theology — Divine Commentary	The Rule of Faith — Apostles' Creed and Nicene Creed	The Lord's Supper — Dramatic Re-enactment	Embodiment — Anamnesis and Prolepsis through the Church Year	Extravagant Generosity — Good Works
Covenant Keeper — Faithful Promisor	Restorer — Christ, the Victor over the powers of evil	Guide — Divine Presence and Shekinah	Spiritual Food — Sustenance for the Journey	The Vincentian Canon — Ubiquity, antiquity, universality	Eschatological Foreshadowing — The Already/Not Yet	Effective Discipling — Spiritual Formation in the Believing Assembly	Evangelical Witness — Making Disciples of All People Groups

Appendix 6

From Before to Beyond Time
The Plan of God and Human History

Adapted from Suzanne de Dietrich. *God's Unfolding Purpose*. Philadelphia: Westminster Press, 1976.

I. Before Time (Eternity Past) 1 Cor. 2.7
   A. The Eternal Triune God
   B. God's Eternal Purpose
   C. The Mystery of Iniquity
   D. The Principalities and Powers

II. Beginning of Time (Creation and Fall) Gen. 1.1
   A. Creative Word
   B. Humanity
   C. Fall
   D. Reign of Death and First Signs of Grace

III. Unfolding of Time (God's Plan Revealed Through Israel) Gal. 3.8
   A. Promise (Patriarchs)
   B. Exodus and Covenant at Sinai
   C. Promised Land
   D. The City, the Temple, and the Throne (Prophet, Priest, and King)
   E. Exile
   F. Remnant

IV. Fullness of Time (Incarnation of the Messiah) Gal. 4.4-5
   A. The King Comes to His Kingdom
   B. The Present Reality of His Reign
   C. The Secret of the Kingdom: the Already and the Not Yet
   D. The Crucified King
   E. The Risen Lord

V. The Last Times (The Descent of the Holy Spirit) Acts 2.16-18
   A. Between the Times: the Church as Foretaste of the Kingdom
   B. The Church as Agent of the Kingdom
   C. The Conflict Between the Kingdoms of Darkness and Light

VI. The Fulfillment of Time (The Second Coming) Matt. 13.40-43
   A. The Return of Christ
   B. Judgment
   C. The Consummation of His Kingdom

VII. Beyond Time (Eternity Future) 1 Cor. 15.24-28
   A. Kingdom Handed Over to God the Father
   B. God as All in All

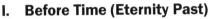

From Before to Beyond Time

Scriptures for Major Outlines Points

I. Before Time (Eternity Past)

1 Cor. 2.7 (ESV) - But we impart a secret and hidden wisdom of God, *which God decreed before the ages* for our glory (cf. Titus 1.2).

II. Beginning of Time (Creation and Fall)

Gen. 1.1 (ESV) - *In the beginning,* God created the heavens and the earth.

III. Unfolding of Time (God's Plan Revealed Through Israel)

Gal. 3.8 (ESV) - And the Scripture, foreseeing that God would justify the Gentiles by faith, *preached the Gospel beforehand to Abraham,* saying, "In you shall all the nations be blessed" (cf. Rom. 9.4-5).

IV. Fullness of Time (The Incarnation of the Messiah)

Gal. 4.4-5 (ESV) - *But when the fullness of time had come,* God sent forth his Son, born of woman, born under the law, to redeem those who were under the law, so that we might receive adoption as sons.

V. The Last Times (The Descent of the Holy Spirit)

Acts 2.16-18 (ESV) - But this is what was uttered through the prophet Joel: "'*And in the last days it shall be,*' God declares, 'that I will pour out my Spirit on all flesh, and your sons and your daughters shall prophesy, and your young men shall see visions, and your old men shall dream dreams; even on my male servants and female servants in those days I will pour out my Spirit, and they shall prophesy.'"

VI. The Fulfillment of Time (The Second Coming)

Matt. 13.40-43 (ESV) - Just as the weeds are gathered and burned with fire, *so will it be at the close of the age.* The Son of Man will send his angels, and they will gather out of his Kingdom all causes of sin and all lawbreakers, and throw them into the fiery furnace. In that place there will be weeping and gnashing of teeth. Then the righteous will shine like the sun in the Kingdom of their Father. He who has ears, let him hear.

VII. Beyond Time (Eternity Future)

1 Cor. 15.24-28 (ESV) - Then comes the end, when he delivers the Kingdom to God the Father after destroying every rule and every authority and power. For he must reign until he has put all his enemies under his feet. The last enemy to be destroyed is death. For "God has put all things in subjection under his feet." But when it says, "all things are put in subjection," it is plain that he is excepted who put all things in subjection under him. When all things are subjected to him, then the Son himself will also be subjected to him who put all things in subjection under him, that God may be all in all.

APPENDIX 7

THE SHADOW AND THE SUBSTANCE
Rev. Dr. Don L. Davis

Song, Aspiration, and Longing in Worship and Devotion

The Righteous Demands of the Old Testament Moral Law

The Patriarchs and the Covenants

Appearances of the Angel of the Lord (Theophanies)

Types and Foreshadowings in People, Places, Things, and Events

The Tabernacle

The Law
(Genesis - Deuteronomy)
Foundation for Christ

History
(Joshua - Esther)
Preparation for Christ

Poetry
(Job - Song of Solomon)
Aspiration for Christ

Prophecy
(Isaiah - Malachi)
Expectation of Christ

Adam and the History of Israel as Recapitulation

Gentile Inclusion in the Salvation of God

Old Testament Messianic Prophecy

Offices of the Prophets, Priesthood, and King

Prophecies Concerning the Kingdom of God

The Temple Sacrifices and Festivals

APPENDIX 8
IN CHRIST
Rev. Dr. Don L. Davis

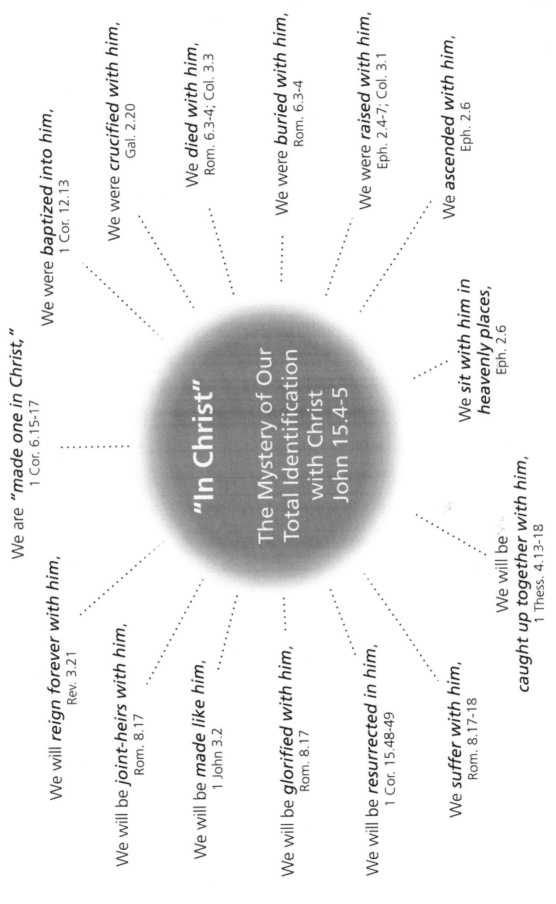

We were **baptized into him,** 1 Cor. 12.13

We were **crucified with him,** Gal. 2.20

We **died with him,** Rom. 6.3-4; Col. 3.3

We were **buried with him,** Rom. 6.3-4

We were **raised with him,** Eph. 2.4-7; Col. 3.1

We **ascended with him,** Eph. 2.6

We **sit with him in heavenly places,** Eph. 2.6

We are "**made one in Christ,**" 1 Cor. 6.15-17

"In Christ"
The Mystery of Our Total Identification with Christ John 15.4-5

We will **reign forever with him,** Rev. 3.21

We will be **joint-heirs with him,** Rom. 8.17

We will be **made like him,** 1 John 3.2

We will be **glorified with him,** Rom. 8.17

We will be **resurrected in him,** 1 Cor. 15.48-49

We **suffer with him,** Rom. 8.17-18

We will be **caught up together with him,** 1 Thess. 4.13-18

Appendix 9

Our Declaration of Dependence: Freedom in Christ
Rev. Dr. Don L. Davis

It is important to teach Christian morality within the realm of the freedom that was won for us by Christ's death on the Cross, and the entrance of the Holy Spirit into the life and mission of the Church (i.e., Galatians 5.1, "It is for freedom Christ has set you free"), and always in the context of using your freedom in the framework of bringing God glory and advancing Christ's Kingdom. Along with some critical texts on freedom in the Epistles, I believe we can equip others to live for Christ and his Kingdom by emphasizing the "6-8-10" principles of 1 Corinthians, and apply them to all moral issues.

1. 1 Cor. 6.9-11 - Christianity is about transformation in Christ; no amount of excuses will get a person into the Kingdom.

2. 1 Cor. 6.12a - We are free in Christ, but not everything one does is edifying or helpful.

3. 1 Cor. 6.12b - We are free in Christ, but anything that is addictive and exercising control over you is counter to Christ and his Kingdom.

4. 1 Cor. 8.7-13 - We are free in Christ, but we ought never to flaunt our freedom, especially in the face of Christians whose conscience would be marred and who would stumble if they see us doing something they find offensive.

5. 1 Cor.10.23 - We are free in Christ; all things are lawful for us, but not everything is helpful, nor does doing everything build oneself up.

6. 1 Cor.10.24 - We are free in Christ, and ought to use our freedom to love our brothers and sisters in Christ, and nurture them for others' well being (cf. Gal. 5.13)

7. 1 Cor. 10.31 - We are free in Christ, and are given that freedom in order that we might glorify God in all that we do, whether we eat or drink, or anything else we do.

8. 1 Cor. 10.32-33 - We are free in Christ, and ought to use our freedom in order to do what we can to give no offense to people in the world or the Church, but do what we do in order to influence them to know and love Christ, i.e., that they might be saved.

In addition to these principles, I believe we ought also to emphasize the following principles:

- 1 Pet. 2.16 – We ought to live free in Christ as servants of God, but never seek to use our freedom as a cover-up for evil.

- John 8.31-32 – We show ourselves to be disciples of Christ as we abide and continue in his Word, and in so doing we come to know the truth, and the truth sets us free in him.

- Gal. 5.13 – As brothers and sisters in Christ, we are called to be free, yet not to use our freedom as a license to indulge our sinful natures; rather, we are called to be free in order to serve one another in love.

This focus on freedom, in my mind, places all things that we say to adults or teens in context. Often, the way in which we disciple many new Christians is through a rigorous taxonomy (listing) of different vices and moral ills, and this can, at times, not only give them the sense that Christianity is an anti-act religion (a religion of simply not doing things), and/or a faith overly concerned with not sinning. Actually, the moral focus in Christianity is on freedom, a freedom won at high price, a freedom to love God and advance the Kingdom, a freedom to live a surrendered life before the Lord. The moral responsibility of urban Christians is to live free in Jesus Christ, to live free unto God's glory, and to not use their freedom from the law as a license for sin.

The core of the teaching, then, is to focus on the freedom won for us through Christ's death and resurrection, and our union with him. We are now set free from the law, the principle of sin and death, the condemnation and guilt of our own sin, and the conviction of the law on us. We serve God now out of gratitude and thankfulness, and the moral impulse is living free in Christ. Yet, we do not use our freedom to be wiseguys or knuckle-heads, but to glorify God and love others. This is the context that addresses the thorny issues of homosexuality, abortion, and other social ills. Those who engage in such acts feign freedom, but, lacking a knowledge of God in Christ, they are merely following their own internal predispositions, which are not informed either by God's moral will or his love.

Freedom in Christ is a banner call to live holy and joyously as urban disciples. This freedom will enable them to see how creative they can be as Christians in the midst of so-called "free" living which only leads to bondage, shame, and remorse.

APPENDIX 10

THE OIKOS FACTOR

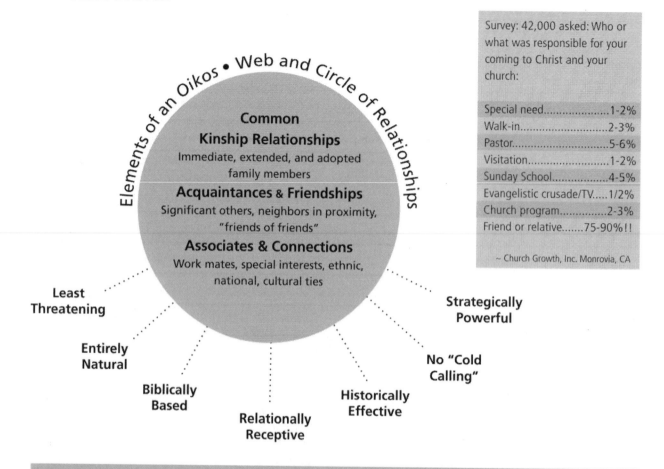

Elements of an Oikos • Web and Circle of Relationships

Common Kinship Relationships
Immediate, extended, and adopted family members

Acquaintances & Friendships
Significant others, neighbors in proximity, "friends of friends"

Associates & Connections
Work mates, special interests, ethnic, national, cultural ties

Least Threatening

Entirely Natural

Biblically Based

Relationally Receptive

Historically Effective

No "Cold Calling"

Strategically Powerful

Survey: 42,000 asked: Who or what was responsible for your coming to Christ and your church:

Special need	1-2%
Walk-in	2-3%
Pastor	5-6%
Visitation	1-2%
Sunday School	4-5%
Evangelistic crusade/TV	1/2%
Church program	2-3%
Friend or relative	75-90%!!

~ Church Growth, Inc. Monrovia, CA

Oikos (household) in the OT
"A household usually contained four generations, including men, married women, unmarried daughters, slaves of both sexes, persons without citizenship, and 'sojourners,' or resident foreign workers."

~ Hans Walter Wolff, Anthology of the Old Testament.

Oikos (household) in the NT
Evangelism and disciple making in our NT narratives are often described as following the flow of the relational networks of various people within their *oikoi* (households), that is, those natural lines of connection in which they resided and lived (c.f., Mark 5.19; Luke 19.9; John 4.53; 1.41-45, etc.). Andrew to Simon (John 1.41-45), and both Cornelius (Acts 10-11) and the Philippian jailer (Acts 16) are notable cases of evangelism and discipling through *oikoi.*

Oikos (household) among the urban poor
While great differences exist between cultures, kinship relationships, special interest groups, and family structures among urban populations, it is clear that urbanites connect with others far more on the basis of connections through relationships, friendships, and family than through proximity and neighborhood alone. Often times the closest friends of urban poor dwellers are not immediately close by in terms of neighborhood; family and friends may dwell blocks, even miles away. Taking the time to study the precise linkages of relationships among the dwellers in a certain area can prove extremely helpful in determining the most effective strategies for evangelism and disciple making in inner city contexts.

APPENDIX 11

THE THEOLOGY OF CHRISTUS VICTOR

Rev. Dr. Don L. Davis

	The Promised Messiah	The Word Made Flesh	The Son of Man	The Suffering Servant	The Lamb of God	The Victorious Conqueror	The Reigning Lord in Heaven	The Bridegroom and Coming King
Biblical Framework	Israel's hope of Yahweh's anointed who would redeem his people	In the person of Jesus of Nazareth, the Lord has come to the world	As the promised king and divine Son of Man, Jesus reveals the Father's glory and salvation to the world	As Inaugurator of the Kingdom of God, Jesus demonstrates God's reign present through his words, wonders, and works	As both High Priest and Paschal Lamb, Jesus offers himself to God on our behalf as a sacrifice for sin	In his resurrection from the dead and ascension to God's right hand, Jesus is proclaimed as Victor over the power of sin and death	Now reigning at God's right hand till his enemies are made his footstool, Jesus pours out his benefits on his body	Soon the risen and ascended Lord will return to gather his Bride, the Church, and consummate his work
Scripture References	Isa. 9.6-7 Jer. 23.5-6 Isa. 11.1-10	John 1.14-18 Matt. 1.20-23 Phil. 2.6-8	Matt. 2.1-11 Num. 24.17 Luke 1.78-79	Mark 1.14-15 Matt. 12.25-30 Luke 17.20-21	2 Cor. 5.18-21 Isa. 52-53 John 1.29	Eph. 1.16-23 Phil. 2.5-11 Col. 1.15-20	1 Cor. 15.25 Eph. 4.15-16 Acts. 2.32-36	Rom. 14.7-9 Rev. 5.9-13 1 Thess. 4.13-18
Jesus' History	The pre-incarnate, only begotten Son of God in glory	His conception by the Spirit, and birth to Mary	His manifestation to the Magi and to the world	His teaching, exorcisms, miracles, and mighty works among the people	His suffering, crucifixion, death, and burial	His resurrection, with appearances to his witnesses, and his ascension to the Father	The sending of the Holy Spirit and his gifts, and Christ's session in heaven at the Father's right hand	His soon return from heaven to earth as Lord and Christ: the Second Coming
Description	The biblical promise for the seed of Abraham, the prophet like Moses, the son of David	In the Incarnation, God has come to us; Jesus reveals to humankind the Father's glory in fullness	In Jesus, God has shown his salvation to the entire world, including the Gentiles	In Jesus, the promised Kingdom of God has come visibly to earth, demonstrating his binding of Satan and rescinding the Curse	As God's perfect Lamb, Jesus offers himself up to God as a sin offering on behalf of the entire world	In his resurrection and ascension, Jesus destroyed death, disarmed Satan, and rescinded the Curse	Jesus is installed at the Father's right hand as Head of the Church, Firstborn from the dead, and supreme Lord in heaven	As we labor in his harvest field in the world, so we await Christ's return, the fulfillment of his promise
Church Year	Advent	Christmas	Season after Epiphany Baptism and Transfiguration	Lent	Holy Week Passion	Eastertide Easter, Ascension Day, Pentecost	Season after Pentecost Trinity Sunday	Season after Pentecost All Saints Day, Reign of Christ the King
	The Coming of Christ	*The Birth of Christ*	*The Manifestation of Christ*	*The Ministry of Christ*	*The Suffering and Death of Christ*	*The Resurrection and Ascension of Christ*	*The Heavenly Session of Christ*	*The Reign of Christ*
Spiritual Formation	As we await his Coming, let us proclaim and affirm the hope of Christ	O Word made flesh, let us every heart prepare him room to dwell	Divine Son of Man, show the nations your salvation and glory	In the person of Christ, the power of the reign of God has come to earth and to the Church	May those who share the Lord's death be resurrected with him	Let us participate by faith in the victory of Christ over the power of sin, Satan, and death	Come, indwell us, Holy Spirit, and empower us to advance Christ's Kingdom in the world	We live and work in expectation of his soon return, seeking to please him in all things

APPENDIX 12

CHRISTUS VICTOR: AN INTEGRATED VISION FOR THE CHRISTIAN LIFE AND WITNESS

Rev. Dr. Don L. Davis

For the Church

- The Church is the primary extension of Jesus in the world
- Ransomed treasure of the victorious, risen Christ
- *Laos:* The people of God
- God's new creation: presence of the future
- Locus and agent of the Already/Not Yet Kingdom

For Theology and Doctrine

- The authoritative Word of Christ's victory: the Apostolic Tradition: the Holy Scriptures
- Theology as commentary on the grand narrative of God
- *Christus Victor* as the core theological framework for meaning in the world
- The Nicene Creed: the Story of God's triumphant grace

For Spirituality

- The Holy Spirit's presence and power in the midst of God's people
- Sharing in the disciplines of the Spirit
- Gatherings, lectionary, liturgy, and our observances in the Church Year
- Living the life of the risen Christ in the rhythm of our ordinary lives

For Gifts

- God's gracious endowments and benefits from *Christus Victor*
- Pastoral offices to the Church
- The Holy Spirit's sovereign dispensing of the gifts
- Stewardship: divine, diverse gifts for the common good

Christus Victor

*Destroyer of Evil and Death
Restorer of Creation
Victor o'er Hades and Sin
Crusher of Satan*

For Worship

- People of the Resurrection: unending celebration of the people of God
- Remembering, participating in the Christ event in our worship
- Listen and respond to the Word
- Transformed at the Table, the Lord's Supper
- The presence of the Father through the Son in the Spirit

For Evangelism and Mission

- Evangelism as unashamed declaration and demonstration of *Christus Victor* to the world
- The Gospel as Good News of kingdom pledge
- We proclaim God's Kingdom come in the person of Jesus of Nazareth
- The Great Commission: go to all people groups making disciples of Christ and his Kingdom
- Proclaiming Christ as Lord and Messiah

For Justice and Compassion

- The gracious and generous expressions of Jesus through the Church
- The Church displays the very life of the Kingdom
- The Church demonstrates the very life of the Kingdom of heaven right here and now
- Having freely received, we freely give (no sense of merit or pride)
- Justice as tangible evidence of the Kingdom come

APPENDIX *13*

UNDERSTANDING THE BIBLE IN PARTS AND WHOLE

Rev. Don Allsman

The Bible is the authoritative account of God's plan to exalt Jesus as Lord of all, redeem all creation, and put down God's enemies forever. The subject of the Bible is Jesus Christ (John 5.39-40):

- The Old Testament is the anticipation and promise of Christ
- The New Testament is the climax and fulfillment in Christ

"In the OT the NT lies hidden; in the NT the OT stands revealed."

Elements of plot development: beginning, rising action, climax, falling action, resolution

1. **Beginning**: Creation and fall of man (the problem and need for resolution), Genesis 1.1 - 3.15

2. **Rising Action**: God's plan revealed through Israel (Genesis 3.15 - Malachi)

3. **Climax**: Jesus inaugurates his Kingdom (Matthew - Acts 1.11)

4. **Falling Action**: The Church continues Jesus' kingdom work (Acts 1.12 - Revelation 3)

5. **Resolution**: Jesus returns to consummate the Kingdom (Revelation 4 - 22)

6. **Commentary**: The people of God describe their experiences to provide wisdom (The Wisdom literature: Job, Psalms, Proverbs, Ecclesiastes, Song of Solomon)

The Bible in book order:

Genesis, Exodus, Leviticus, Numbers, Deuteronomy, Joshua, Judges, Ruth, 1-2 Samuel	History from Creation to the reign of King David
1-2 Kings	Israel's history from David to Exile
1-2 Chronicles	Various historical accounts from Creation to Exile
Ezra, Nehemiah, Esther	Accounts of Israel in Exile and return
Job (contemporary of Abraham), Psalms (primarily of David), Proverbs, Ecclesiastes, Song of Solomon (Solomon's time)	Wisdom literature
Isaiah, Jeremiah, Lamentation, Ezekiel, Daniel, Hosea, Amos, Obadiah, Jonah, Micah, Nahum, Habakkuk, Zephaniah, Haggai, Zechariah, Malachi	Writings of Israel's prophets from the time of the Kings through the return from Exile
Matthew, Mark, Luke, John	The account of Jesus of Nazareth (Gospels)
Acts, Romans, 1-2 Corinthians, Galatians, Ephesians, Philippians, Colossians, 1-2 Thessalonians, 1-2 Timothy, Titus, Philemon, Hebrews, James, 1-2 Peter, 1-3 John, Jude, Revelation	The account of the Church after Jesus' ascension, including letters of apostolic instruction to the Church (Epistles)
Revelation	The future and the end of the age (Jesus' return)

APPENDIX 14

THIRTY-THREE BLESSINGS IN CHRIST

Rev. Dr. Don L. Davis

Did you know that 33 things happened to you at the moment you became a believer in Jesus Christ? Lewis Sperry Chafer, the first president of Dallas Theological Seminary, listed these benefits of salvation in his *Systematic Theology, Volume III* (pp. 234-266). These points, along with brief explanations, give the born-again Christian a better understanding of the work of grace accomplished in his/her life as well as a greater appreciation of his/her new life.

1. In the eternal plan of God, the believer is:

    a. *Foreknown* - Acts 2.23; 1 Pet. 1.2, 20. God knew from all eternity every step in the entire program of the universe.

    b. *Predestined* - Rom. 8.29-30. A believer's destiny has been appointed through foreknowledge to the unending realization of all God's riches of grace.

    c. *Elected* - Rom. 8.38; Col. 3.12. He/she is chosen of God in the present age and will manifest the grace of God in future ages.

    d. *Chosen* - Eph. 1.4. God has separated unto himself his elect who are both foreknown and predestined.

    e. *Called* - 1 Thess. 6.24. God invites man to enjoy the benefits of his redemptive purposes. This term may include those whom God has selected for salvation, but who are still in their unregenerate state.

2. A believer has been *redeemed* - Rom. 3.24. The price required to set him/her free from sin has been paid.

3. A believer has been *reconciled* - 2 Cor. 6.18, 19; Rom. 5.10. He/she is both restored to fellowship by God and restored to fellowship with God.

4. A believer is related to God through *propitiation* - Rom. 3.24-26. He/she has been set free from judgment by God's satisfaction with his Son's death for sinners.

5. A believer has been *forgiven* all trespasses - Eph. 1.7. All his/her sins are taken care of - past, present, and future.

6. A believer is vitally **conjoined to Christ** for the judgment of the old man "unto a new walk" - Rom. 6.1-10. He/she is brought into a union with Christ.

7. A believer is *"free from the law"* - Rom. 7.2-6. He/she is both dead to its condemnation, and delivered from its jurisdiction.

8. A believer has been made a **child of God** - Gal. 3.26. He/she is born anew by the regenerating power of the Holy Spirit into a relationship in which God the First Person becomes a legitimate Father and the saved one becomes a legitimate child with every right and title - an heir of God and a joint heir with Jesus Christ.

9. A believer has been **adopted as an adult child** into the Father's household - Rom. 8.15, 23.

10. A believer has been **made acceptable to God** by Jesus Christ - Eph. 1.6. He/she is made **righteous** (Rom. 3.22), **sanctified** (set apart) positionally (1 Cor. 1.30, 6.11); **perfected forever in his/her standing and position** (Heb. 10.14), and **made acceptable** in the Beloved (Col. 1.12).

11. A believer has been **justified** - Rom. 5.1. He/she has been declared righteous by God's decree.

12. A believer is *"made right"* - Eph. 2.13. A close relation is set up and exists between God and the believer.

13. A believer has been **delivered from the power of darkness** - Col. 1.13; 2.13. A Christian has been delivered from Satan and his evil spirits. Yet the disciple must continue to wage warfare against these powers.

14. A believer has been **translated into the Kingdom of God** - Col. 1.13. The Christian has been transferred from Satan's kingdom to Christ's Kingdom.

15. A believer is **planted** on the Rock, Jesus Christ - 1 Cor. 3.9-15. Christ is the foundation on which the believer stands and on which he/she builds his/her Christian life.

16. A believer is a **gift from God to Jesus Christ** - John 17.6, 11, 12, 20. He/she is the Father's love gift to Jesus Christ.

17. A believer is **circumcised in Christ** - Col. 2.11. He/she has been delivered from the power of the old sin nature.

18. A believer has been made a ***partaker of the Holy and Royal Priesthood*** - 1 Pet. 2.5, 9. He/she is a priest because of his/her relation to Christ, the High Priest, and will reign on earth with Christ.

19. A believer is part of a ***chosen generation, a holy nation and a peculiar people*** - 1 Pet. 2.9. This is the company of believers in this age.

20. A believer is a ***heavenly citizen*** - Phil. 3.20. Therefore he/she is called a stranger as far as his/her life on earth is concerned (1 Pet. 2.13), and will enjoy his/her true home in heaven forever.

21. A believer is in ***the family and household of God*** - Eph. 2.1, 9. He/she is part of God's "family" which is composed only of true believers.

22. A believer is in ***the fellowship of the saints*** - John 17.11, 21-23. He/she can be a part of the fellowship of believers with one another.

23. A believer is in ***a heavenly association*** - Col. 1.27; 3.1; 2 Cor. 6.1; Col. 1.24; John 14.12-14; Eph. 5.25-27; Titus 2.13. He/she is a partner with Christ now in life, position, service, suffering, prayer, betrothal as a bride to Christ, and expectation of the coming again of Christ.

24. A believer has ***access to God*** - Eph. 2.18. He/she has access to God's grace which enables him/her to grow spiritually, and he/she has unhindered approach to the Father (Heb. 4.16).

25. A believer is within ***the "much more" care of God*** - Rom. 5.8-10. He/she is an object of God's love (John 3.16), God's grace (Eph. 2.7-9), God's power (Eph. 1.19), God's faithfulness (Phil. 1.6), God's peace (Rom. 5.1), God's consolation (2 Thess. 2.16-17), and God's intercession (Rom. 8.26).

26. A believer is ***God's inheritance*** - Eph. 1.18. He/she is given to Christ as a gift from the Father.

27. A believer ***has the inheritance of God himself*** and all that God bestows - 1 Pet. 1.4.

28. A believer has ***light in the Lord*** - 2 Cor. 4.6. He/she not only has this light, but is commanded to walk in the light.

29. A believer is ***vitally united to the Father, the Son and the Holy Spirit*** - 1 Thess. 1.1; Eph. 4.6; Rom. 8.1; John 14.20; Rom. 8.9; 1 Cor. 2.12.

30. A believer is blessed with ***the earnest or firstfruits of the Spirit*** - Eph. 1.14; 8.23. He/she is born of the Spirit (John 3.6), and baptized by the

Spirit (1 Cor. 12.13), which is a work of the Holy Spirit by which the believer is joined to Christ's body and comes to be "in Christ," and therefore is a partaker of all that Christ is. The disciple is also indwelt by the Spirit (Rom. 8.9), sealed by the Spirit (2 Cor. 1.22), making him/her eternally secure, and filled with the Spirit (Eph. 5.18) whose ministry releases his power and effectiveness in the heart in which he dwells.

31. A believer is **glorified** - Rom. 8.18. He/she will be a partaker of the infinite story of the Godhead.

32. A believer is **complete in God** - Col. 2.9, 10. He/she partakes of all that Christ is.

33. A believer **possesses every spiritual blessing** - Eph. 1.3. All the riches tabulated in the other 32 points made before are to be included in this sweeping term, "all spiritual blessings."

APPENDIX 15

THE HUMP
Rev. Dr. Don L. Davis

The Mature Christian
The Mature Believer and the Spiritual Disciplines

Faithful Application

Gracefulness

Automatic response

Comfortableness

Personal Satisfaction

Excellence

Expertise

Training Others

Heart Desire
A Clear Goal
Feasible Plan
Solid Support
Correct Knowledge
Faithful Effort
Good Examples
Extended Period of Time
Longsuffering

Regular, correct application of the spiritual disciplines

The Baby Christian
The New Believer and the Spiritual Disciplines

Awkwardness

Unskillfulness

Mistakes

Roughness

Sporadic Behavior

Uncomfortableness

Inefficiency

Novice-Level Performance

APPENDIX 16

GOING FORWARD BY LOOKING BACK
Toward an Evangelical Retrieval of the Great Tradition

Rev. Dr. Don L. Davis

Rediscovering the "Great Tradition"

In a wonderful little book, Ola Tjorhom,[1] describes the Great Tradition of the Church (sometimes called the "classical Christian tradition") as "living, organic, and dynamic."[2] The Great Tradition represents that evangelical, apostolic, and catholic core of Christian faith and practice which came largely to fruition from 100-500 AD.[3] Its rich legacy and treasures represent the Church's confession of what the Church has always believed, the worship that the ancient, undivided Church celebrated and embodied, and the mission that it embraced and undertook.

While the Great Tradition neither can substitute for the Apostolic Tradition (i.e., the authoritative source of all Christian faith, the Scriptures), nor should it overshadow the living presence of Christ in the Church through the Holy Spirit, it is still authoritative and revitalizing for the people of God. It has and still can provide God's people through time with the substance of its confession and faith. The Great Tradition has been embraced and affirmed as authoritative by Catholic, Orthodox, Anglican, and Protestant theologians, those ancient and modern, as it has produced the seminal documents, doctrines, confessions, and practices of the Church (e.g., the canon of Scriptures, the doctrines of the Trinity, the deity of Christ, etc.).

. . . .

[1] Ola Tjorhom, *Visible Church–Visible Unity: Ecumenical Ecclesiology and "The Great Tradition of the Church."* Collegeville, Minnesota: Liturgical Press, 2004. Robert Webber defined the Great Tradition in this way: "[It is] the broad outline of Christian belief and practice developed from the Scriptures between the time of Christ and the middle of the fifth century." Robert E. Webber, *The Majestic Tapestry*. Nashville: Thomas Nelson Publishers, 1986, p. 10.

[2] *Ibid.*, p. 35.

[3] The core of the Great Tradition concentrates on the formulations, confessions, and practices of the Church's first five centuries of life and work. Thomas Oden, in my judgment, rightly asserts that ". . . . most of what is enduringly valuable in contemporary biblical exegesis was discovered by the fifth century" (cf. Thomas C. Oden, *The Word of Life*. San Francisco: HarperSanFrancisco, 1989, p. xi.).

Many evangelical scholars today believe that the way forward for dynamic faith and spiritual renewal will entail looking back, not with sentimental longings for the "good old days" of a pristine, problem-free early church, or a naive and even futile attempt to ape their heroic journey of faith. Rather, with a critical eye to history, a devout spirit of respect for the ancient Church, and a deep commitment to Scripture, we ought to rediscover through the Great Tradition the seeds of a new, authentic, and empowered faith. We can be transformed as we retrieve and are informed by the core beliefs and practices of the Church before the horrible divisions and fragmentations of Church history.

Well, if we do believe we ought to at least look again at the early Church and its life, or better yet, are convinced even to retrieve the Great Tradition for the sake of renewal in the Church–what exactly are we hoping to get back? Are we to uncritically accept everything the ancient Church said and did as "gospel," to be truthful simply because it is closer to the amazing events of Jesus of Nazareth in the world? Is old "hip," in and of itself?

No. We neither accept all things uncritically, nor do we believe that old, in and of itself, is truly good. Truth for us is more than ideas or ancient claims; for us, truth was incarnated in the person of Jesus of Nazareth, and the Scriptures give authoritative and final claim to the meaning of his revelation and salvation in history. We cannot accept things simply because they are reported to have been done in the past, or begun in the past. Amazingly, the Great Tradition itself argued for us to be critical, to contend for the faith once delivered to the saints (Jude 3), to embrace and celebrate the tradition received from the Apostles, rooted and interpreted by the Holy Scriptures themselves, and expressed in Christian confession and practice.

Core Dimensions of the Great Tradition

While Tjorhom offers his own list of ten elements of the theological content of the Great Tradition that he believes is worthy of reinterpretation and regard,[4] I believe there are seven dimensions that, from a biblical and spiritual vantage point, can enable us to understand what the early Church believed, how they worshiped and lived, and the ways they defended their living faith in Jesus Christ. Through their allegiance to the documents, confessions, and practices of this period, the ancient Church bore witness to God's salvation promise in the midst of a pagan and crooked generation.

. . . .

[4] *Ibid.*, pp. 27-29. Tjorhom's ten elements are argued in the context of his work where he also argues for the structural elements and the ecumenical implications of retrieving the Great Tradition. I wholeheartedly agree with the general thrust of his argument, which, like my own belief, makes the claim that an interest in and study of the Great Tradition can renew and enrich the contemporary Church in its worship, service, and mission.

The core of our current faith and practice was developed in this era, and deserves a second (and twenty-second) look.

Adapting, redacting, and extending Tjorhom's notions of the Great Tradition, I list here what I take to be, as a start, a simple listing of the critical dimensions that deserve our undivided attention and wholehearted retrieval.

1. ***The Apostolic Tradition.*** The Great Tradition is rooted in the Apostolic Tradition, i.e., the apostles' eyewitness testimony and firsthand experience of Jesus of Nazareth, their authoritative witness to his life and work recounted in the Holy Scriptures, the canon of our Bible today. The Church is apostolic, built on the foundation of the prophets and the apostles, with Christ himself being the Cornerstone. The Scriptures themselves represent the source of our interpretation about the Kingdom of God, that story of God's redemptive love embodied in the promise to Abraham and the patriarchs, in the covenants and experience of Israel, and which culminates in the revelation of God in Christ Jesus, as predicted in the prophets and explicated in the apostolic testimony.

2. ***The Ecumenical Councils and Creeds, Especially the Nicene Creed.*** The Great Tradition declares the truth and sets the bounds of the historic orthodox faith as defined and asserted in the ecumenical creeds of the ancient and undivided Church, with special focus on the Nicene Creed. Their declarations were taken to be an accurate interpretation and commentary on the teachings of the apostles set in Scripture. While not the source of the Faith itself, the confession of the ecumenical councils and creeds represents the *substance of its teachings*,[5] especially those before the fifth century (where virtually all of the elemental doctrines concerning God, Christ, and salvation were articulated and embraced).[6]

. . . .

[5] I am indebted to the late Dr. Robert E. Webber for this helpful distinction between the source and the substance of Christian faith and interpretation.

[6] While the seven ecumenical Councils (along with others) are affirmed by both Catholic and Orthodox communions as binding, it is the first four Councils that are to be considered the critical, most essential confessions of the ancient, undivided Church. I and others argue for this largely because the first four articulate and settle once and for all what is to be considered our orthodox faith on the doctrines of the Trinity and the Incarnation (cf. Philip Schaff, *The Creeds of Christendom*, v. 1. Grand Rapids: Baker Book House, 1996, p. 44). Similarly, even the magisterial Reformers embraced the teaching of the Great Tradition, and held its most significant confessions as authoritative. Correspondingly, Calvin could argue in his own theological interpretations that "Thus

3. ***The Ancient Rule of Faith.*** The Great Tradition embraced the substance of this core Christian faith in a rule, i.e., an ancient standard rule of faith, that was considered to be the yardstick by which claims and propositions regarding the interpretation of the biblical faith were to be assessed. This rule, when applied reverently and rigorously, can clearly allow us to define the core Christian confession of the ancient and undivided Church expressed clearly in that instruction and adage of Vincent of Lerins: "that which has always been believed, everywhere, and by all."[7]

4. ***The Christus Victor Worldview.*** The Great Tradition celebrates and affirms Jesus of Nazareth as the Christ, the promised Messiah of the Hebrew Scriptures, the risen and exalted Lord, and Head of the Church. In Jesus of Nazareth alone, God has reasserted his reign over the universe, having destroyed death in his dying, conquering God's enemies through his incarnation, death, resurrection, and ascension, and ransoming humanity from its penalty due to its transgression of the Law. Now resurrected from the dead, ascended and exalted at the right hand of God, he has sent the Holy Spirit into the world to empower the Church in its life and witness. The Church is to be considered the people of the victory of Christ. At his return, he will consummate his work as Lord. This worldview was expressed in the ancient Church's confession, preaching, worship, and witness. Today, through its liturgy and practice of the Church Year, the Church acknowledges, celebrates,

---

councils would come to have the majesty that is their due; yet in the meantime Scripture would stand out in the higher place, with everything subject to its standard. In this way, we willingly embrace and reverence as holy the early councils, such as those of Nicea, Constantinople, the first of Ephesus I, Chalcedon, and the like, which were concerned with refuting errors—in so far as they relate to the teachings of faith. For they contain nothing but the pure and genuine exposition of Scripture, which the holy Fathers applied with spiritual prudence to crush the enemies of religion who had then arisen" (cf. John Calvin, *Institutes of the Christian Religion*, IV, ix. 8. John T. McNeill, ed. Ford Lewis Battles, trans. Philadelphia: Westminster Press, 1960, pp. 1171-72).

[7] This rule, which has won well-deserved favor down through the years as a sound theological yardstick for authentic Christian truth, weaves three cords of critical assessment to determine what may be counted as orthodox or not in the Church's teaching. St. Vincent of Lerins, a theological commentator who died before 450 AD, authored what has come to be called the "Vincentian canon, a three-fold test of catholicity: *quod ubique, quod semper, quod ab omnibus creditum est* (what has been believed everywhere, always and by all). By this three-fold test of ecumenicity, antiquity, and consent, the church may discern between true and false traditions." (cf. Thomas C. Oden, *Classical Pastoral Care*, vol. 4. Grand Rapids: Baker Books, 1987, p. 243).

embodies, and proclaims this victory of Christ: the destruction of sin and evil and the restoration of all creation.

5. ***The Centrality of the Church.*** The Great Tradition confidently confessed the Church as the people of God. The faithful assembly of believers, under the authority of the Shepherd Christ Jesus, is now the locus and agent of the Kingdom of God on earth. In its worship, fellowship, teaching, service, and witness, Christ continues to live and move. The Great Tradition insists that the Church, under the authority of its undershepherds and the entirety of the priesthood of believers, is visibly the dwelling of God in the Spirit in the world today. With Christ himself being the Chief Cornerstone, the Church is the temple of God, the body of Christ, and the temple of the Holy Spirit. All believers, living, dead, and yet unborn–make up the one, holy, catholic (universal), and apostolic community. Gathering together regularly in believing assembly, members of the Church meet locally to worship God through Word and sacrament, and to bear witness in its good works and proclamation of the Gospel. Incorporating new believers into the Church through baptism, the Church embodies the life of the Kingdom in its fellowship, and demonstrates in word and deed the reality of the Kingdom of God through its life together and service to the world.

6. ***The Unity of the Faith.*** The Great Tradition affirms unequivocally the catholicity of the Church of Jesus Christ, in that it is concerned with keeping communion and continuity with the worship and theology of the Church throughout the ages (Church universal). Since there has been and can only be one hope, calling, and faith, the Great Tradition fought and strove for oneness in word, in doctrine, in worship, in charity.

7. ***The Evangelical Mandate of the Risen Christ.*** The Great Tradition affirms the apostolic mandate to make known to the nations the victory of God in Jesus Christ, proclaiming salvation by grace through faith in his name, and inviting all peoples to repentance and faith to enter into the Kingdom of God. Through acts of justice and righteousness, the Church displays the life of the Kingdom in the world today, and through its preaching and life together provides a witness and sign of the Kingdom present in and for the world (*sacramentum mundi*), and as the pillar and ground of the truth. As evidence of the Kingdom of God and custodians of the Word of God, the Church is charged to define clearly and defend the faith once for all delivered to the Church by the apostles.

Conclusion: Finding Our Future by Looking Back

In a time where so many are confused by the noisy chaos of so many claiming to speak for God, it is high time for us to rediscover the roots of our faith, to go back to the beginning of Christian confession and practice, and see, if in fact, we can recover our identity in the stream of Christ worship and discipleship that changed the world. In my judgment, this can be done through a critical, evangelical appropriation of the Great Tradition, that core belief and practice which is the source of all our traditions, whether Catholic, Orthodox, Anglican, or Protestant.

Of course, specific traditions will continue to seek to express and live out their commitment to the Authoritative Tradition (i.e., the Scriptures) and Great Tradition through their worship, teaching, and service. Our diverse Christian traditions (little "t"), when they are rooted in and expressive of the teaching of Scripture and led by the Holy Spirit, will continue to make the Gospel clear within new cultures or sub-cultures, speaking and modeling the hope of Christ into new situations shaped by their own set of questions posed in light of their own unique circumstances. Our traditions are essentially movements of contextualization, that is they are attempts to make plain within people groups the Authoritative Tradition in a way that faithfully and effectively leads them to faith in Jesus Christ.

We ought, therefore, to find ways to enrich our contemporary traditions by reconnecting and integrating our contemporary confessions and practices with the Great Tradition. Let us never forget that Christianity, at its core, is a faithful witness to God's saving acts in history. As such, we will always be a people who seek to find our futures by looking back through time at those moments of revelation and action where the Rule of God was made plain through the incarnation, passion, resurrection, ascension, and soon-coming of Christ. Let us then remember, celebrate, reenact, learn afresh, and passionately proclaim what believers have confessed since the morning of the empty tomb—the saving story of God's promise in Jesus of Nazareth to redeem and save a people for his own.

Appendix 17

Summary Outline of the Scriptures

Rev. Dr. Don L. Davis

The Old Testament

1. **Genesis** – *Beginnings*
   a. Adam
   b. Noah
   c. Abraham
   d. Isaac
   e. Jacob
   f. Joseph

2. **Exodus** – *Redemption (out of)*
   a. Slavery
   b. Deliverance
   c. Law
   d. Tabernacle

3. **Leviticus** – *Worship and Fellowship*
   a. Offerings and sacrifices
   b. Priests
   c. Feasts and festivals

4. **Numbers** – *Service and Walk*
   a. Organized
   b. Wanderings

5. **Deuteronomy** – *Obedience*
   a. Moses reviews history and law
   b. Civil and social laws
   c. Palestinian Covenant
   d. Moses' blessing and death

6. **Joshua** – *Redemption (into)*
   a. Conquer the land
   b. Divide up the land
   c. Joshua's farewell

7. **Judges** – *God's Deliverance*
   a. Disobedience and judgment
   b. Israel's twelve judges
   c. Lawless conditions

8. **Ruth** – *Love*
   a. Ruth chooses
   b. Ruth works
   c. Ruth waits
   d. Ruth rewarded

9. **1 Samuel** – *Kings, Priestly Perspective*
   a. Eli
   b. Samuel
   c. Saul
   d. David

10. **2 Samuel** – *David*
    a. King of Judah (9 years - Hebron)
    b. King of all Israel (33 years - Jerusalem)

11. **1 Kings** – *Solomon's Glory, Kingdom's Decline*
    a. Solomon's glory
    b. Kingdom's decline
    c. Elijah the prophet

12. **2 Kings** – *Divided Kingdom*
    a. Elisha
    b. Israel (Northern Kingdom falls)
    c. Judah (Southern Kingdom falls)

13. **1 Chronicles** – *David's Temple Arrangements*
    a. Genealogies
    b. End of Saul's reign
    c. Reign of David
    d. Temple preparations

14. **2 Chronicles** – *Temple and Worship Abandoned*
    a. Solomon
    b. Kings of Judah

15. **Ezra** – *The Minority (Remnant)*
    a. First return from exile - Zerubbabel
    b. Second return from exile - Ezra (priest)

16. **Nehemiah** – *Rebuilding by Faith*
    a. Rebuild walls
    b. Revival
    c. Religious reform

17. **Esther** – *Female Savior*
    a. Esther
    b. Haman
    c. Mordecai
    d. Deliverance: Feast of Purim

18. **Job** – *Why the Righteous Suffer*
    a. Godly Job
    b. Satan's attack
    c. Four philosophical friends
    d. God lives

19. **Psalms** – *Prayer and Praise*
    a. Prayers of David
    b. Godly suffer; deliverance
    c. God deals with Israel
    d. Suffering of God's people - end with the Lord's reign
    e. The Word of God (Messiah's suffering and glorious return)

20. **Proverbs** – *Wisdom*
    a. Wisdom vs. folly
    b. Solomon
    c. Solomon - Hezekiah
    d. Agur
    e. Lemuel

21. **Ecclesiastes** – *Vanity*
    a. Experimentation
    b. Observation
    c. Consideration

22. **Song of Solomon** – *Love Story*

23. **Isaiah** – *The Justice (Judgment) and Grace (Comfort) of God*
    a. Prophecies of punishment
    b. History
    c. Prophecies of blessing

24. **Jeremiah** – *Judah's Sin Leads to Babylonian Captivity*
    a. Jeremiah's call; empowered
    b. Judah condemned; predicted Babylonian captivity
    c. Restoration promised
    d. Prophesied judgment inflicted
    e. Prophecies against Gentiles
    f. Summary of Judah's captivity

25. **Lamentations** – *Lament over Jerusalem*
    a. Affliction of Jerusalem
    b. Destroyed because of sin
    c. The prophet's suffering
    d. Present desolation vs. past splendor
    e. Appeal to God for mercy

26. **Ezekiel** – *Israel's Captivity and Restoration*
    a. Judgment on Judah and Jerusalem
    b. Judgment on Gentile nations
    c. Israel restored; Jerusalem's future glory

27. **Daniel** – *The Time of the Gentiles*
    a. History; Nebuchadnezzar, Belshazzar, Daniel
    b. Prophecy

28. **Hosea** – *Unfaithfulness*
    a. Unfaithfulness
    b. Punishment
    c. Restoration

29. **Joel** – *The Day of the Lord*
    a. Locust plague
    b. Events of the future Day of the Lord
    c. Order of the future Day of the Lord

30. **Amos** – *God Judges Sin*
    a. Neighbors judged
    b. Israel judged
    c. Visions of future judgment
    d. Israel's past judgment blessings

31. **Obadiah** – *Edom's Destruction*
    a. Destruction prophesied
    b. Reasons for destruction
    c. Israel's future blessing

32. **Jonah** – *Gentile Salvation*
    a. Jonah disobeys
    b. Others suffer
    c. Jonah punished
    d. Jonah obeys; thousands saved
    e. Jonah displeased, no love for souls

33. **Micah** – *Israel's Sins, Judgment, and Restoration*
    a. Sin and judgment
    b. Grace and future restoration
    c. Appeal and petition

34. **Nahum** – *Nineveh Condemned*
    a. God hates sin
    b. Nineveh's doom prophesied
    c. Reasons for doom

35. **Habakkuk** – *The Just Shall Live by Faith*
    a. Complaint of Judah's unjudged sin
    b. Chaldeans will punish
    c. Complaint of Chaldeans' wickedness
    d. Punishment promised
    e. Prayer for revival; faith in God

36. **Zephaniah** – *Babylonian Invasion Prefigures the Day of the Lord*
    a. Judgment on Judah foreshadows the Great Day of the Lord
    b. Judgment on Jerusalem and neighbors foreshadows final judgment of all nations
    c. Israel restored after judgments

37. **Haggai** – *Rebuild the Temple*
    a. Negligence
    b. Courage
    c. Separation
    d. Judgment

38. **Zechariah** – *Two Comings of Christ*
    a. Zechariah's vision
    b. Bethel's question; Jehovah's answer
    c. Nation's downfall and salvation

39. **Malachi** – *Neglect*
    a. The priest's sins
    b. The people's sins
    c. The faithful few

The New Testament

1. **Matthew** – *Jesus the King*
   a. The Person of the King
   b. The Preparation of the King
   c. The Propaganda of the King
   d. The Program of the King
   e. The Passion of the King
   f. The Power of the King

2. **Mark** – *Jesus the Servant*
   a. John introduces the Servant
   b. God the Father identifies the Servant
   c. The temptation initiates the Servant
   d. Work and word of the Servant
   e. Death burial, resurrection

3. **Luke** – *Jesus Christ the Perfect Man*
   a. Birth and family of the Perfect Man
   b. Testing of the Perfect Man; hometown
   c. Ministry of the Perfect Man
   d. Betrayal, trial, and death of the Perfect Man
   e. Resurrection of the Perfect Man

4. **John** – *Jesus Christ is God*
   a. Prologue - the Incarnation
   b. Introduction
   c. Witness of works and words
   d. Witness of Jesus to his apostles
   e. Passion - witness to the world
   f. Epilogue

5. **Acts** – *The Holy Spirit Working in the Church*
   a. The Lord Jesus at work by the Holy Spirit through the apostles at Jerusalem
   b. In Judea and Samaria
   c. To the uttermost parts of the Earth

6. **Romans** – *The Righteousness of God*
   a. Salutation
   b. Sin and salvation
   c. Sanctification
   d. Struggle
   e. Spirit-filled living
   f. Security of salvation
   g. Segregation
   h. Sacrifice and service
   i. Separation and salutation

7. **1 Corinthians** – *The Lordship of Christ*
   a. Salutation and thanksgiving
   b. Conditions in the Corinthian body
   c. Concerning the Gospel
   d. Concerning collections

8. **2 Corinthians** – *The Ministry of the Church*
   a. The comfort of God
   b. Collection for the poor
   c. Calling of the Apostle Paul

9. **Galatians** – *Justification by Faith*
   a. Introduction
   b. Personal - Authority of the apostle and glory of the Gospel
   c. Doctrinal - Justification by faith
   d. Practical - Sanctification by the Holy Spirit
   e. Autographed conclusion and exhortation

10. **Ephesians** – *The Church of Jesus Christ*
    a. Doctrinal - the heavenly calling of the Church
       - A Body
       - A Temple
       - A Mystery
    b. Practical - the earthly conduct of the Church
       - A New Man
       - A Bride
       - An Army

11. **Philippians** – *Joy in the Christian Life*
    a. Philosophy for Christian living
    b. Pattern for Christian living
    c. Prize for Christian living
    d. Power for Christian living

12. **Colossians** – *Christ the Fullness of God*
    a. Doctrinal - Christ, the fullness of God; in Christ believers are made full
    b. Practical - Christ, the fullness of God; Christ's life poured out in believers, and through them

13. **1 Thessalonians** – *The Second Coming of Christ:*
    a. Is an inspiring hope
    b. Is a working hope
    c. Is a purifying hope
    d. Is a comforting hope
    e. Is a rousing, stimulating hope

14. **2 Thessalonians** – *The Second Coming of Christ*
    a. Persecution of believers now; judgment of unbelievers hereafter (at coming of Christ)
    b. Program of the world in connection with the coming of Christ
    c. Practical issues associated with the coming of Christ

15. **1 Timothy** – *Government and Order in the Local Church*
    a. The faith of the Church
    b. Public prayer and women's place in the Church
    c. Officers in the Church
    d. Apostasy in the Church
    e. Duties of the officer of the Church

16. **2 Timothy** – *Loyalty in the Days of Apostasy*
    a. Afflictions of the Gospel
    b. Active in service
    c. Apostasy coming; authority of the Scriptures
    d. Allegiance to the Lord

17. **Titus** – *The Ideal New Testament Church*
    a. The Church is an organization
    b. The Church is to teach and preach the Word of God
    c. The Church is to perform good works

18. **Philemon** – *Reveal Christ's Love and Teach Brotherly Love*
    a. Genial greeting to Philemon and family
    b. Good reputation of Philemon
    c. Gracious plea for Onesimus
    d. Guiltless substitutes for guilty
    e. Glorious illustration of imputation
    f. General and personal requests

19. **Hebrews** – *The Superiority of Christ*
    a. Doctrinal - Christ is better than the Old Testament economy
    b. Practical - Christ brings better benefits and duties

20. **James** – *Ethics of Christianity*
    a. Faith tested
    b. Difficulty of controlling the tongue
    c. Warning against worldliness
    d. Admonitions in view of the Lord's coming

21. **1 Peter** – *Christian Hope in the Time of Persecution and Trial*
    a. Suffering and security of believers
    b. Suffering and the Scriptures
    c. Suffering and the sufferings of Christ
    d. Suffering and the Second Coming of Christ

22. **2 Peter** – *Warning against False Teachers*
    a. Addition of Christian graces gives assurance
    b. Authority of the Scriptures
    c. Apostasy brought in by false testimony
    d. Attitude toward return of Christ: test for apostasy
    e. Agenda of God in the world
    f. Admonition to believers

23. **1 John** – *The Family of God*
    a. God is light
    b. God is love
    c. God is life

24. **2 John** – *Warning against Receiving Deceivers*
    a. Walk in truth
    b. Love one another
    c. Receive not deceivers
    d. Find joy in fellowship

25. **3 John** – *Admonition to Receive True Believers*
    a. Gaius, brother in the Church
    b. Diotrephes
    c. Demetrius

26. **Jude** – *Contending for the Faith*
    a. Occasion of the epistle
    b. Occurrences of apostasy
    c. Occupation of believers in the days of apostasy

27. **Revelation** – *The Unveiling of Christ Glorified*
    a. The person of Christ in glory
    b. The possession of Jesus Christ - the Church in the World
    c. The program of Jesus Christ - the scene in Heaven
    d. The seven seals
    e. The seven trumpets
    f. Important persons in the last days
    g. The seven vials
    h. The fall of Babylon
    i. The eternal state

Appendix 18

CHRONOLOGICAL TABLE OF THE NEW TESTAMENT

Robert Yarbrough

Date	Christian History	NT	Roman History
c. 28-30	Public ministry of Jesus	Gospels	14-37, Tiberious, emperor
c. 33	Conversion of Paul	Acts 9.1-13	—
c. 35	Paul's first post-conversion Jerusalem visit	Gal. 1.18	—
c. 35-46	Paul in Cilicia and Syria	Gal. 1.21	—
—	—	—	c. 37-41, Gaius, emperor c. 41-54, Claudius, emperor
c. 46	Paul's second Jerusalem visit	Gal. 2.1; Acts 11.27-50	—
c. 47-48	Paul and Barnabas in Cyprus and Galatia (1st Journey)	Acts 13-14	—
c. 48?	Letter to the Galatians	—	—
c. 49	Council of Jerusalem	Acts 15	—
c. 49-50	Paul and Silas from Syrian Antioch through Asia Minor to Macedonia and Achaia (2nd Journey)	Acts 15.36-18.21	—
c. 50	Letters to the Thessalonians	—	—
c. 50-52	Paul in Corinth	—	c. 51-52, Gallio, proconsul of Achaia
Summer 52	Paul's third Jerusalem visit	—	c. 52-59, Felix, procurator of Judea
c. 52-55	Paul in Ephesus	—	c. 54-68, Nero, emperor
c. 55-56	Letters to the Corinthians	—	—
c. 55-57	Paul in Macedonia, Illyricum, and Achaia (3rd Journey)	Acts 18.22-21.15	—
Early 57	Letter to the Romans	—	—
May 57	Paul's fourth (and last) Jerusalem visit	Acts 21.17	
c. 57-59	Paul's imprisonment in Caesarea	Acts 23.23	c. 59, Festus succeeds Felix as procurator of Judea
Sept. 59	Paul's voyage to Rome begins	Acts 27-28	—
Feb. 60	Paul's arrival in Rome	—	—
c. 60-62	Paul's house arrest in Rome	—	—
c. 60-62?	Captivity Letters (Ephesians, Philippians, Colossians, Philemon)	—	c. 62, death of Festus; Albinus procurator of Judea
c. 65?	Paul visits Spain (4th Journey?)	—	c. 64, Fire of Rome
c. ??	Pastoral Letters (1 and 2 Timothy, Titus)	—	—
c. 65?	Death of Paul	—	—

COMMUNICATING MESSIAH: THE RELATIONSHIP OF THE GOSPELS

Adapted from N. R. Ericson and L. M. Perry. *John: A New Look at the Fourth Gospel*

	Matthew	Mark	Luke	John
Date	c. 65	c. 59	c. 61	c. 90
Chapters	28	16	24	21
Verses	1,071	666	1,151	879
Period	36 years	4 years	37 years	4 years
Audience	The Jews	The Romans	The Greeks	The World
Christ As	The King	The Servant	The Man	The Son of God
Emphasis	Sovereignty	Humility	Humanity	Deity
Sign	The Lion	The Ox	The Man	The Eagle
Ending	Resurrection	Empty Tomb	Promise of the Spirit	Promise of His Second Coming
Written In	Antioch?	Rome	Rome	Ephesus
Key Verse	27.37	10.45	19.10	20.30-31
Key Word	Kingdom	Service	Salvation	Believe
Purpose	Presentation of Jesus Christ		Interpretation of Jesus the Messiah	
Time to Read	2 hours	1 1/4 hours	2 1/4 hours	1 1/2 hours

FIT TO REPRESENT: MULTIPLYING DISCIPLES OF THE KINGDOM OF GOD

Rev. Dr. Don L. Davis

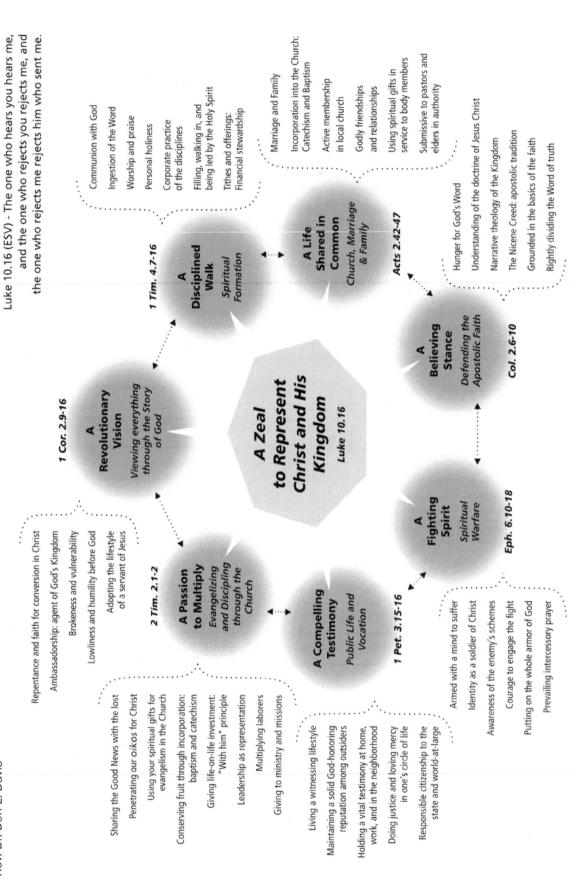

Luke 10.16 (ESV) - The one who hears you hears me, and the one who rejects you rejects me, and the one who rejects me rejects him who sent me.

A Zeal to Represent Christ and His Kingdom
Luke 10.16

A Disciplined Walk
Spiritual Formation
1 Tim. 4.7-16

- Communion with God
- Ingestion of the Word
- Worship and praise
- Personal holiness
- Corporate practice of the disciplines
- Filling, walking in, and being led by the Holy Spirit
- Tithes and offerings: Financial stewardship

A Life Shared in Common
Church, Marriage & Family
Acts 2.42-47

- Marriage and Family
- Incorporation into the Church: Catechism and Baptism
- Active membership in local church
- Godly friendships and relationships
- Using spiritual gifts in service to body members
- Submissive to pastors and elders in authority

A Believing Stance
Defending the Apostolic Faith
Col. 2.6-10

- Hunger for God's Word
- Understanding of the doctrine of Jesus Christ
- Narrative theology of the Kingdom
- The Nicene Creed: apostolic tradition
- Grounded in the basics of the faith
- Rightly dividing the Word of truth

A Revolutionary Vision
Viewing everything through the Story of God
1 Cor. 2.9-16

- Repentance and faith for conversion in Christ
- Ambassadorship: agent of God's Kingdom
- Brokeness and vulnerability
- Lowliness and humility before God
- Adopting the lifestyle of a servant of Jesus

A Passion to Multiply
Evangelizing and Discipling through the Church
2 Tim. 2.1-2

- Sharing the Good News with the lost
- Penetrating our *oikos* for Christ
- Using your spiritual gifts for evangelism in the Church
- Conserving fruit through incorporation: baptism and catechism
- Giving life-on-life investment: "With him" principle
- Leadership as representation
- Multiplying laborers
- Giving to ministry and missions

A Compelling Testimony
Public Life and Vocation
1 Pet. 3.15-16

- Living a witnessing lifestyle
- Maintaining a solid God-honoring reputation among outsiders
- Holding a vital testimony at home, work, and in the neighborhood
- Doing justice and loving mercy in one's circle of life
- Responsible citizenship to the state and world-at-large

A Fighting Spirit
Spiritual Warfare
Eph. 6.10-18

- Armed with a mind to suffer
- Identity as a soldier of Christ
- Awareness of the enemy's schemes
- Courage to engage the fight
- Putting on the whole armor of God
- Prevailing intercessory prayer

APPENDIX 21

ETHICS OF THE NEW TESTAMENT
Living in the Upside-Down Kingdom of God

Rev. Dr. Don L. Davis

The Principle of Reversal

The Principle Expressed	Scripture
The poor shall become rich, and the rich shall become poor	Luke 6.20-26
The law breaker and the undeserving are saved	Matt. 21.31-32
Those who humble themselves shall be exalted	1 Pet. 5.5-6
Those who exalt themselves shall be brought low	Luke 18.14
The blind shall be given sight	John 9.39
Those claiming to see shall be made blind	John 9.40-41
We become free by being Christ's slave	Rom. 12.1-2
God has chosen what is foolish in the world to shame the wise	1 Cor. 1.27
God has chosen what is weak in the world to shame the strong	1 Cor. 1.27
God has chosen the low and despised to bring to nothing things that are	1 Cor. 1.28
We gain the next world by losing this one	1 Tim. 6.7
Love this life and you'll lose it; hate this life, and you'll keep the next	John 12.25
You become the greatest by being the servant of all	Matt. 10.42-45
Store up treasures here, you forfeit heaven's reward	Matt. 6.19
Store up treasures above, you gain heaven's wealth	Matt. 6.20
Accept your own death to yourself in order to live fully	John 12.24
Release all earthly reputation to gain heaven's favor	Phil. 3.3-7
The first shall be last, and the last shall become first	Mark 9.35
The grace of Jesus is perfected in your weakness, not your strength	2 Cor. 12.9
God's highest sacrifice is contrition and brokenness	Ps. 51.17
It is better to give to others than to receive from them	Acts 20.35
Give away all you have in order to receive God's best	Luke 6.38

APPENDIX 22

Jesus Christ, the Subject and Theme of the Bible

Rev. Dr. Don L. Davis

Adapted from Norman Geisler, *A Popular Survey of the Old Testament*. Grand Rapids, MI: Baker Books, 1977, pp. 11ff

Jesus Christ, the Subject and Theme of the Bible — Luke 24.27, 44; Heb. 10.7; Matt. 5.17; John 5.39	Two-fold Structure of the Bible	Four-fold Structure of the Bible	Eight-fold Structure of the Bible
	Old Testament: Anticipation Concealed Contained The precept In shadow In ritual In picture As foretold In prophecy In Pre-incarnations	**The Law** *Foundation for Christ*	**The Law:** Foundation for Christ (Genesis-Deuteronomy)
			History: Preparation for Christ (Joshua-Esther)
		The Prophets *Expectation of Christ*	**Poetry:** Aspiration for Christ (Job-Song of Solomon)
			Prophets: Expectation of Christ (Isaiah-Malachi)
	New Testament: Realization Revealed Explained Its perfection In substance In reality In person As fulfilled In history In the Incarnation	**The Gospels** *Manifestation of Christ*	**Gospels:** Manifestation of Christ (Matthew-John)
			Acts: Propagation of Christ (The Acts of the Apostles)
		The Epistles *Interpretation of Christ*	**Epistles:** Interpretation of Christ (Romans-Jude)
			Revelation: Consummation in Christ (The Revelation of John)

APPENDIX 23

LET GOD ARISE!
The Seven "A's" of Seeking the Lord and Entreating His Favor

Rev. Dr. Don L. Davis

#		THEME	SCRIPTURE	AWARENESS		CONCERT OF PRAYER
1	Adoration	• Delight and Enjoyment in God • Overwhelming Gratefulness • Acknowledging God in his Person and Works	Ps. 29.1-2 Rev. 4-11 Rom. 11.33-36 Ps. 27.4-8	Of God's Majestic Glory		Gather to Worship and Pray
2	Admission	• Powerlessness • Helplessness • Awareness of One's Desperate Need for God	Ps. 34.18-19 Prov. 28.13 Dan. 4.34-35 Isa. 30.1-5	Of Our Brokenness before God	God's Face	Confess Your Powerlessness
3	Availability	• Dying to preoccupation with self and love of the world • No confidence in fleshly wisdom, resources, or method • Consecrating ourselves as living sacrifices to God	Rom. 12.1-5 John 12.24 Phil. 3.3-8 Gal. 6.14	Of Our Yieldedness to God		Surrender Your All to Christ
4	Awakening *Global and Local*	• Refreshment: outpouring of the Holy Spirit on God's people • Renewal: Obedience to the Great Commandment - Loving God and neighbor • Revolution: Radical new orientation to Christ as Lord	Hos. 6.1-3 Eph. 3.15-21 Matt. 22.37-40 John 14.15	Asking for the Spirit's Filling	Fullness	Fervently Intercede on Behalf of Others
5	Advancement *Global and Local*	• Movements: outreaches to unreached, pioneer regions • Mobilization: of every assembly to fulfill the Great Commission • Military mindset: Adopting a warfare mentality to suffer and endure hardness in spiritual warfare	Acts 1.8 Mark 16.15-16 Matt. 28.18-20 Matt. 11.12 Luke 19.41-42 2 Tim. 2.1-4	Asking for the Spirit's Moving	Fulfillment	
6	Affirmation	• Giving Testimony over what the Lord has done • Challenging one another by speaking the truth in Love	Ps. 107.1-2 Heb. 3.13 2 Cor. 4.13 Mal. 3.16-18	The Redeemed Saying So	The Faith	Encourage One Another in Truth and Testimony
7	Acknowledgment	• Waiting patiently on God to act by his timing and methods • Living confidently as though God is answering our petitions • Acting as if God will do precisely what he says he will do	Ps. 27.14 2 Chron. 20.12 Prov. 3.5-6 Isa. 55.8-11 Ps. 2.8	Keeping Our Eyes on the Lord	The Fight	Scatter to Work and Wait

"Seek the Lord"
Zechariah 8.18-23 • Isaiah 55.6

"Entreat the Favor of the Lord"
Zechariah 8.18-23 • Jeremiah 33.3

Appendix 24

The Nicene Creed

We believe in one God, the Father Almighty, maker of heaven and earth and of all things visible and invisible.

We believe in one Lord Jesus Christ, the only begotten Son of God, begotten of the Father before all ages, God from God, Light from Light, True God from True God, begotten not created, of the same essence as the Father, through whom all things were made.

Who for us men and for our salvation came down from heaven and was incarnate by the Holy Spirit and the virgin Mary and became human. Who for us too, was crucified under Pontius Pilate, suffered and was buried. The third day he rose again according to the Scriptures, ascended into heaven and is seated at the right hand of the Father. He will come again in glory to judge the living and the dead, and his Kingdom will have no end.

We believe in the Holy Spirit, the Lord and life-giver, who proceeds from the Father and the Son. Who together with the Father and Son is worshiped and glorified. Who spoke by the prophets.

We believe in one holy, catholic, and apostolic church.

We acknowledge one baptism for the forgiveness of sin, and we look for the resurrection of the dead and the life of the age to come. Amen.

Appendix 25

THE NICENE CREED
With Biblical Support

The Urban Ministry Institute

We believe in one God, *(Deut. 6.4-5; Mark 12.29; 1 Cor. 8.6)*
    the Father Almighty, *(Gen. 17.1; Dan. 4.35; Matt. 6.9; Eph. 4.6; Rev. 1.8)*
    Maker of heaven and earth *(Gen. 1.1; Isa. 40.28; Rev. 10.6)*
    and of all things visible and invisible. *(Ps. 148; Rom. 11.36; Rev. 4.11)*

We believe in one Lord Jesus Christ, the only Begotten Son of God, begotten of the Father
    before all ages, God from God, Light from Light, True God from True God, begotten not
    created, of the same essence as the Father,
        (John 1.1-2; 3.18; 8.58; 14.9-10; 20.28; Col. 1.15, 17; Heb. 1.3-6)
    through whom all things were made. *(John 1.3; Col. 1.16)*

Who for us men and for our salvation came down from heaven and was incarnate by the Holy
    Spirit and the Virgin Mary and became human.
        (Matt. 1.20-23; John 1.14; 6.38; Luke 19.10)
    Who for us too, was crucified under Pontius Pilate, suffered and was buried.
        (Matt. 27.1-2; Mark 15.24-39, 43-47; Acts 13.29; Rom. 5.8; Heb. 2.10; 13.12)
    The third day he rose again according to the Scriptures,
        (Mark 16.5-7; Luke 24.6-8; Acts 1.3; Rom. 6.9; 10.9; 2 Tim. 2.8)
    ascended into heaven, and is seated at the right hand of the Father.
        (Mark 16.19; Eph. 1.19-20)
    He will come again in glory to judge the living and the dead, and his Kingdom will have no
    end. *(Isa. 9.7; Matt. 24.30; John 5.22; Acts 1.11; 17.31; Rom. 14.9; 2 Cor. 5.10; 2 Tim. 4.1)*

We believe in the Holy Spirit, the Lord and life-giver, *(Gen. 1.1-2; Job 33.4; Ps. 104.30; 139.7-8;*
    Luke 4.18-19; John 3.5-6; Acts 1.1-2; 1 Cor. 2.11; Rev. 3.22)
    who proceeds from the Father and the Son, *(John 14.16-18, 26; 15.26; 20.22)*
    who together with the Father and Son is worshiped and glorified,
        (Isa. 6.3; Matt. 28.19; 2 Cor. 13.14; Rev. 4.8)
    who spoke by the prophets. *(Num. 11.29; Mic. 3.8; Acts 2.17-18; 2 Pet. 1.21)*

We believe in one holy, catholic, and apostolic Church.
    (Matt. 16.18; Eph. 5.25-28; 1 Cor. 1.2; 10.17; 1 Tim. 3.15; Rev. 7.9)

We acknowledge one baptism for the forgiveness of sin, *(Acts 22.16; 1 Pet. 3.21; Eph. 4.4-5)*
    And we look for the resurrection of the dead and the life of the age to come.
    (Isa. 11.6-10; Mic. 4.1-7; Luke 18.29-30; Rev. 21.1-5; 21.22-22.5)
    Amen.

The Nicene Creed with Biblical Support – Memory Verses

Below are suggested memory verses, one for each section of the Creed.

The Father

Rev. 4.11 (ESV) – Worthy are you, our Lord and God, to receive glory and honor and power, for you created all things, and by your will they existed and were created.

The Son

John 1.1 (ESV) – In the beginning was the Word, and the Word was with God, and the Word was God.

The Son's Mission

1 Cor. 15.3-5 (ESV) – For what I received I passed on to you as of first importance: that Christ died for our sins according to the Scriptures, that he was buried, that he was raised on the third day according to the Scriptures, and that he appeared to Peter, and then to the Twelve.

The Holy Spirit

Rom. 8.11 (ESV) – If the Spirit of him who raised Jesus from the dead dwells in you, he who raised Christ Jesus from the dead will also give life to your mortal bodies through his Spirit who dwells in you.

The Church

1 Pet. 2.9 (ESV) – But you are a chosen race, a royal priesthood, a holy nation, a people for his own possession, that you may proclaim the excellencies of him who called you out of darkness into his marvelous light.

Our Hope

1 Thess. 4.16-17 (ESV) – For the Lord himself will descend from heaven with a cry of command, with the voice of an archangel, and with the sound of the trumpet of God. And the dead in Christ will rise first. Then we who are alive, who are left, will be caught up together with them in the clouds to meet the Lord in the air, and so we will always be with the Lord.

APPENDIX 26

THE APOSTLES' CREED

I believe in God, the Father Almighty, Maker of heaven and earth; and in Jesus Christ his only Son, our Lord; who was conceived by the Holy Spirit, born of the Virgin Mary, suffered under Pontius Pilate, was crucified, dead, and buried; he descended into hell; the third day he arose again from the dead; he ascended into heaven and sits on the right hand of God the Father Almighty; from thence he shall come to judge the quick and the dead.

I believe in the Holy Spirit, the holy catholic church, the communion of saints, the forgiveness of sins, the resurrection of the body, and the life everlasting. Amen.

Made in the USA
Columbia, SC
15 July 2018